Griffin's Fire

(Book Two)

Darby Karchut

Copper Square Studios

Griffin's Fire

This is a work of fiction. All concepts, characters and events portrayed in this book are used fictitiously and any resemblance to real people or events is purely coincidental.

Copyright © 2012 Darby Karchut

All rights reserved. No part of this book may be reproduced, stored in a retrieval system or transmitted in any form by any means electronic, mechanical, photocopying, recording or otherwise, except brief extracts for the purpose of review, without the permission of the publisher and copyright owner.

Copper Square Studios
Colorado Springs, Colorado

First Edition, August 2014
Library of Congress Cataloging-in-Publication Data pending

Karchut, Darby
Griffin's Fire : a novel / by Darby Karchut -- 1st ed.
p. cm.

Summary:
Forced to become mortal, a sixteen year-old ex-teen angel must deal with the heaven-and-hell known as high school while struggling to get along with his Mentor's new apprentice.

Cover design by Wes Karchut

ISBN 978-0-9741145-0-7 (paperback)
ISBN 978-0-9741145-9-0 (e-book)

(originally published 2012 by Twilight Times Books)

Printed in the United States of America

praise for

Griffin's Fire (Book Two)

"I adore this series beyond reason." -- *Kellyvision*

"An amazing storyteller, Darby Karchut has once again mesmerized me with characters powerful and witty..."-- Jennifer Murgia, author of *Angel Star* and *Forest of Whispers*

"Griffin's Fire is an compelling read that leaves you so excited that you just want more."-- *Books with Bite*

"Karchut does a good job with her teen-friendly prose, and her voice is fresh and engaging."--*The Seattle PI*

As always, to Wes.
Thanks for keeping my feet on the Earth
and the Fire in my heart.

*The Manuscript of Aidan, Abbot of Kellsfarne
In the Year of Our Lord 1144*

Of all spiritual beings, Angels are most sublime. As far as the heavens are above the earth, Angels are above all other spirits. They are reflections of the Divine Thinker and exist to do His bidding alone. As Messengers and Warriors, they are peerless.

Nine choirs there are of Angels: Seraphim, Cherubim, Thrones, the Virtues, the Powers, the Dominions, Principalities, Archangels, and Angels..

However, there exist other spiritual beings, of which we know little. Rumors abound of a lowly caste known as the Terrae Angeli. A dim shadow of Heavenly Angelic powers and strengths, Terrae Angeli exist only to serve as guardians to man. Four ranks have they: Sage, Guardian, Mentor, and Tiro.

*This we know of Terrae Angeli:
Being earthbound, their powers are limited.
Being earthbound, they mirror man in all ways, even unto free will.
Being earthbound, their appearances and powers align to the Four Elements: Wind & Water, Earth & Fire.
Being earthbound, they can destroy and be destroyed.*

Translation from the original Latin:
Professor Julian Fitzwilliam
Oxford
1898

Chapter One

Struggling up the snow covered slope, Griffin post-holed through another drift, his legs growing heavier with each step. Around him, the storm worsened into a blizzard. He cringed when a blast of wind bent a nearby aspen almost in half; with an explosive crack, it snapped off and crash to the ground.

He slowed when he reached a dark stand of pines, grateful for their shelter from the wind. After catching his breath, he lifted his head.

"Basil?" he shouted. "Where are you?" He paused to listen, then raised his hand and snapped his fingers; flames sprang from the tips like miniature torches. They danced and flickered in the gusts swirling through the grove. He lifted his arm higher, trying to catch a glimpse of his Mentor. For some reason, the gloom ate the light from his Fire. "Yeah, real useful, angel boy," he muttered to himself. He gave up. Making a fist, he extinguished the flames and continued through the trees.

A shape loomed ahead in the dusk. He stopped and peered more closely. "Basil?"

A few yards away, the Mentor stood on a fallen log; his cropped, white hair ghostly in the fading light. He motioned for Griffin to hold his position.

"Wait there, lad," Basil called, his words fading in and out as the tempest raged around them. "Wait and I will return for you."

"What do you mean? Why can't I come with you?" Griffin shouted back; he flinched when another gust blew snow into his eyes. He looked again. His Mentor was gone.

"Basil!" Griffin started forward, then tripped on a hidden rock. Flailing his arms, he fell sideways into a snow bank. He slid a few inches down the slope and sank into a warm softness.

For a moment, he laid there, trying to figure out why the warm softness felt like a quilt.

His quilt.

Griffin blinked awake.

Sitting up, he looked around his bedroom in confusion, his heart thundering against his ribs. He pushed his dark hair off his forehead as he licked his lips, tasting sweat. The dream teased at him.

Maybe, just maybe, he thought and held his hand up in front of his face. He hesitated. *Don't be such a wimp—just do it already.* He swallowed and flicked the tip of his forefinger against his thumb.

Nothing happened.

Well, what did you expect? sneered a voice in his head. *A freaking miracle?*

"Shut up," he mumbled to the voice. Or the Voice, as he referred to it. The Voice that was always with him. Constantly reminding him that every tragedy in his life was his own fault. That somehow, in some way, he always deserved it.

Griffin scrubbed at his face. He started to lie back down, then paused at the knock outside his room. "I'm fine, Basil," he called hoarsely. *Go away, Basil. Stop being such a mommy, Basil.*

The door swung open with a creak. The Mentor stepped inside, still belting his robe around his tall frame. "Fin? Are you all right?" He walked over and took a seat next to Griffin.

"Yeah. Why do you ask?"

"Well, could it be because I was just wrenched out a peaceful sleep by my Tiro shouting for me in the dead of night?" His amusement faded when Griffin muttered something. "I beg your pardon?"

"I *said* I'm not your apprentice. Not anymore." The words spilled out of Griffin's mouth before he could stop them.

Cold filled the room. Basil sat frozen for a moment, his face unreadable in the dark. "Right." He stood up. "Well, good night, then." Without another word, he walked out of the room and closed the door behind him.

As the sound of footsteps faded away, Griffin fell back with a groan and pulled the covers over his head.

Griffin's Journal: Monday, January 3rd

I had a dream last night. Kind of a weird one, but at least I was a Terrae Angelus. I had my powers back and everything. I could *feel* the Fire on my fingers. And even though the dream didn't make any sense, it felt awesome to be *me* again.

Then I woke up.

And, God forgive me, but I wish I hadn't.

Because no matter how much I hope and pray, I'm never going to be an angel.

Again.

* * *

Griffin hit the save button on his laptop. Standing up, he kicked the desk chair out of his way, then shuffled over to his bed and flopped backwards onto the rumpled quilt. He made a face when Basil called from his bedroom down the hall.

"Fin, Lena will be here shortly. Are you presentable?"

"Yeah." He glanced down at his stained tee shirt, then pulled it to his nose and sniffed. "I guess."

"Good, because…" Basil's voice trailed off as he appeared in the doorway. His eyes traveled from Griffin's unwashed hair to his bare feet. "Have you even showered today?"

"Why? I'm not going anywhere." Griffin reached over and grabbed his cell phone from the nightstand. "Thanks to Flight Command," he said with a curl of his lip, "I'm grounded for life." He began scrolling down the screen.

Basil tightened his jaw. He stepped over and plucked the device from Griffin's hand.

"Hey!" Griffin squawked. "I was right in the middle of—"

"Lena will be here in ten minutes. I want you washed up before she arrives. You may have *this* back later."

"How later?"

"When I've decided. For now, you are to—"

"But I told Katie I'd call her before dinner."

"I'm sure she'll understand if you wait to—"

"But I need to call her NOW!" Griffin sat up, his eyes flashing with a brown fire.

Basil raised an eyebrow. "And I need to hear a little more civility in your tone of voice. I expect you to be dressed and downstairs in five minutes." Slipping the phone into his pocket, Basil turned around and left.

Griffin stared at the empty doorway. Rage swelled his chest and flooded his mouth. His face twisting with fury, he rolled off his bed and stomped over to the door.

Then slammed it as hard as he could.

Darby Karchut

Chapter Two

Lena Weiss raised the iron knocker and rapped twice, then cocked her head to listen. Furious voices bled through the door of the old house and out into the dusk. *Mein Gott, not another quarrel. I don't know who's carrying more of a burden, Basil with his guilt or Griffin with his anger.*

She knocked again, then gave up and let herself in. Pausing in the foyer, she removed her hat from her gray curls and hung it on a hook; the argument thundered along overhead. She sighed as she pulled off her gloves and unbuttoned her coat.

"…ever slam that door again, you'll be doing extra chores for a month," she heard Basil roar from upstairs.

"Go ahead." Griffin's voice cracked as he shouted back. "I'm stuck here in this stupid house every day anyway. It'll give me something to do."

"As I recall, you chose to stay home. I offered to enroll you in high school and you pitched a royal fit about it."

"Basil?" Lena called, folding her coat on the entryway bench.

"Oh, yeah, that'd be *real* fun. Go to school with a bunch of humans. With Katie there watching me screw up. Good thinking, *Mentor*."

"Basil?" Lena said louder as she walked down the hall to the foot of the stairs. Laying her hand on the newel post for balance, she gazed upward.

"*Mentor* is right. Angel or mortal, you are still my responsibility. Whether you like it or not."

"Well, sorry you're stuck with me." Lena grieved at the faint quiver in Griffin's voice. "Maybe you should've taken Guardian Mayla's suggestion and dumped me with that foster family up in Denver. Not too late, you know."

"That is *not* what I am saying."

"Basil!" Lena resorted to shouting. Silence filled the house for a minute.

"We'll be down directly, Lena. Or at least, I will."

She shook her head at the now muted voices hissing at each other. Stepping across the hallway into the living room, she took a seat in her favorite chair by the fireplace. The flames cackled like mockery. She looked up at the sound of footsteps coming closer.

"My apologies," Basil said a moment later as he walked through the archway into the room. Distress etched lines in his rugged face. "I assume you heard us?"

"I did."

"Anything and everything sets him off. I never know when the next explosion will occur."

"But you understand why he's acting this way, yes?"

Basil slumped down on the nearby sofa with a sigh. "Of course I do. He's hurting and he's angry. And frightened." He propped his head back and gazed up at the ceiling beams. "And it's my fault."

"You must stop blaming yourself. It does him no good—"

"And just who should I blame?" Basil jumped up and stalked over to the window. He glared at his image in the dark glass as he spoke over his shoulder. "Nicopolis? Who simply seized the opportunity to take his revenge against Griffin and me? The Guardians? Mayla and Sukalli were only following our ancient laws."

He whirled around, his blue eyes full of remorse. "I promised him, Lena. After I rescued him from that hell and took him on as my apprentice, as my Tiro; I promised Griffin no one would ever hurt him again. That I would train him and see him through his

Darby Karchut

Proelium, and that he would become a full-fledged Terrae Angelus." Basil jammed his hands into his jeans pockets and looked away. "And then I failed him."

Basil's Journal: Monday, January 3rd

I had another appalling clash with Griffin earlier this evening. I'm afraid we both lost our tempers. For different reasons. Lena came by to offer moral support, but she doesn't know what to do either. We both believe going to school with Katie would be the best thing for him. He needs to accept his mortality and start learning to live with humans. As a human.

Of course he wouldn't even be in this position if it weren't for me. How could I have let this happen? All he ever wanted to be was a Terrae Angelus.

And he would have been such a brilliant guardian angel. Griffin is clever and resourceful and the finest Earth and Fire apprentice I've ever had.

Now he must take that drive and turn it into becoming a decent young man. And I must find a way to help him do so.

Chapter Three

Griffin rested an elbow on the kitchen table, his chin cupped in his hand and one bare foot hooked around the chair leg. The overhead light threw his shadow across the newspaper in front of him. Twirling a pencil between his fingers, he scanned the classified section. *I wish Basil would let me get my own car. Now that I'm permanently earthbound.* He circled an ad, then another. *Of course, after our fight yesterday evening, he probably wouldn't even let me have a tricycle.* He stared blankly at the page in front of him as their latest argument looped through his head.

I wish I hadn't said that about not being his apprentice anymore. What if he decides to get another one? What am I supposed to do then? He promised me that this will always be my home. And that we would always be a family. I hope he really meant it.

He rolled his eyes at his qualms. *It's Basil, dude*, he told himself. *The guy eats and breathes honor—if he makes a promise, he keeps it. Hasn't he always?*

Shaking his head clear, he stretched his arms over his head and arched his back with a pop, then checked the clock. *I wonder if I should go ahead and eat or wait for him.* At an ominous hiss, he jerked his head around. "Oh, Fire!" he cursed.

Griffin leaped across the kitchen to the stove and snatched the pot off the burner. Beef stew oozed over the sides of the hot pan. "I do this every time," he grumbled. He picked up a spoon and scraped at the charred mess, then made a face when he sampled it.

No way are we eating this crap—Basil will think I'm trying to poison him. He carried the ruined dinner over to the sink and flipped on the faucet. As the steam began rising, he squeezed half a bottle of dish soap into the pan.

A gust of wind rattled the panes in the kitchen window.

Griffin froze, his brown eyes wide as he stared at his distorted reflection in the darkened glass. His pulse began to race. After a moment, he turned off the water and tilted his head to one side, listening.

Dripping water in the sink vied with the *tick-ticking* of the cooling stove. The sounds set his teeth on edge.

Without warning, a memory stabbed him. A memory of crouching next to the seeping water heater in the depths of his former Mentor's house, like the depths of hell, nauseous with hopeless fear. Of flinching in rhythm with each *tip-clump, tip-clump* of polished wingtips as Mentor Nicopolis walked down the wooden stairs to the basement, his cold voice promising pain.

Griffin squeezed his eyes shut; his knuckles whitened as he clutched the lip of the sink. He took a deep breath. The smell of burnt stew and lemon soap stung his nose and mouth. He took another breath, trying to calm himself. To focus on the Light as Basil had taught him during their first months together.

I can't do it, Mentor Basil. I can't find it. There's no Light inside of me.

Why, lad, of course, there is. How do you think you were able to survive that monster for three years? Oh, your Light may flicker occasionally, like the flame of a candle, but it's there. Never doubt that.

But I still get scared. Sometimes, I wake up at night and I think I'm...I'm back there with him.

Then seek the Light, Fin, when you are frightened. About anything. It's always present when you need it and it will never fail you.

BOOM!

Griffin's heart leaped into his throat at the sound of a fist hammering the front door. Wiping his hands on his jeans, he hurried out of the kitchen and across the shadowy living room to the front windows. He edged aside the drapes and peeked out.

A huge figure stood under the porch light, his head a scant inch from the rafters. Griffin's stomach knotted. *What's he want now? To finish the job and kill me outright this time?*

As he watched, Guardian Sukalli rocked back on the heels of his cowboy boots. "I know you're there, little brother," he said to the front door. "Are you going to invite me in?"

"Heck, no," Griffin muttered, his breath ghosting the window. "But it's not like I could stop you." He dropped the drape and walked around to the entryway, the tile floor cold under his bare feet. He hesitated, then opened the door.

For a long minute, they stared at each other, the only sound the whisper of the hawk feather fluttering in the night breeze as it dangled from Sukalli's black ponytail. Griffin pressed his lips into a thin line and took a stance in the doorway, furious at his knees for shaking.

"Evening, Griffin."

"Basil's not here."

"Who says I'm here to see Basil?" Sukalli started forward. He paused when Griffin refused to give ground. "You still see me as the villain, don't you, pup?" He pushed past. After shrugging off his fringed buckskin jacket, he hung it on a coat hook over the bench. "Well, I don't blame you. Since I was the one who helped Guardian Mayla *de-angel* you, after all." Peering down, he narrowed his eyes. "How's the whole mortal thing going, anyway?"

Griffin ignored the question as he closed the door. "So what do you want?" he asked, trying to keep his voice steady. He lingered by the archway as Sukalli sauntered into the living room and clicked on a lamp next to the sofa.

"Well, for one thing—I want you to relax. I'm not here to hurt you. Or Basil. I simply wanted to let you know…well, something you should know." His black eyes flickered over to the unlit hearth. "How about a fire first?" He pointed his fingers. Tongues of flames

Darby Karchut

erupted out of their tips and licked the logs; they blazed up with a whoosh. Sukalli gave a satisfied nod. "That's better—things were getting *frosty* in here," he joked. The glow from the fire reflected off the side of his bronze face.

Griffin's heart twisted as he recognized a familiar shape in the form of an earring dangling from one of Sukalli's earlobes. Made from beaten gold wire and crafted into a spiraled diamond, the ancient symbol of Earth flicked in and out of view as it caught the light.

After a minute, the Guardian gestured to a nearby chair. "Sit down, boy. You look like a rabbit being stalked."

"I'm good."

"Suit yourself." Sukalli sat down on the sofa and leaned back. "As you probably know, at Basil's request, I've been looking into—" He paused when the front door banged open. "Speaking of Diablo."

Basil appeared in the doorway. Griffin sighed in relief and edged backwards into the hallway as the Mentor stepped inside. Their eyes met.

"All right, lad?"

Griffin nodded. "Sukalli's here," he said in an undertone.

"Apparently," Basil replied, spying Sukalli's jacket as he hung up his own.

"He says he wants to talk with us about something he's been looking into."

Basil nodded absently. He gazed at Griffin for a few moments, and then straightened as if reaching a decision. "Fin, I want you in your room."

"But I want to—"

"This is not a debate; it's an order."

"But, Basil—"

"Move." Basil gave him a push toward the stairs. "And close your door." He waited until Griffin stomped up the steps and shut his door with a thump. Then he turned and stepped into the living room. He locked eyes with the Guardian.

"Sukalli."

"Basil."

"Pardon my bluntness, but what the bloody hell are you doing here?"

Sukalli rose to his feet. "What is it with you two? You act like I'm—"

"Like you're the one who wouldn't listen to me? The one who refused to believe that Nicopolis lied? Would that be the one?"

"Do you think we *wanted* to do that to the boy?" Sukalli clenched his fists. "But it is the law. *Our* law. And if a Tiro cannot pass his *Proelium*, then…" His voice trailed off.

"Then he's tossed aside. Rejected. Forced to become mortal." Basil shook his head in disgust. "And we call ourselves angels."

Sukalli blew out a long breath. "This is getting us nowhere," he said. "Look, Basil. I'm not here to debate ancient traditions. I *am* here to update you about Nicopolis. Will you at least hear me out before you *throw* me out?"

Basil's jaw twitched. "Right," he said after a moment. He gestured for Sukalli to resume his seat. Choosing a nearby chair, he sat down. "I'm listening."

"I did what you asked. I talked with Flight Command about the entire situation."

"And?"

"And they gave me the go-ahead to question Nicopolis."

"What did you determine?"

"That you were right. Nicopolis probably lied. There were just too many discrepancies between his story, Griffin's account, and your description of the testing site afterward." He raised a hand, forestalling Basil's outburst. "In my opinion, Nicopolis is becoming as loco as a coyote under a full moon. He's obsessed with the belief that you two are out to ruin his reputation. Maybe even ruin his chance at becoming a Guardian." Sukalli grimaced. "He's just as arrogant now as he was when we were all Tiros. I can see why you two had so many brawls. Which he usually lost. He hates your guts, you know."

"I'm aware." *Which is why he jumped at the chance to harm Griffin. Knowing it would hurt me, too*, thought Basil. "Please go on."

"Right after I questioned him, he put in a request to be temporarily taken off rotation and then high-tailed it out of town. No one has heard from him for days which makes him look even more suspicious. So Command is sending me after him. They've decided that he's to be Searched by Mayla."

"What?" Basil bolted upright in his chair. "She agreed to that? I thought she vowed she'd never read another Terrae Angelus' mind again."

"Mayla feels guilty about what happened to Griffin. She's trying to make amends."

"But none of this will help *him*, will it?"

"No, brother. I'm afraid not. But Command has decided that if Nicopolis lied about the *Proelium*, he could be facing severe disciplinary actions."

"Well, it's about bloody time."

"Are you going to tell Griffin about all this?"

Basil thought for a minute. "No, not right now. I'll wait until more time has passed and he has accepted his mortality. Until he finds contentment and purpose as a human."

"I think that's a mistake, but I'll go along with you."

"Thank you. And I'm afraid I must apologize to you. I was rather rude to you earlier."

"Shucks, you're just concerned about the pup. I would be, too, if he were my apprentice." Sukalli grinned, his teeth a white flash in his bronze face. He rose to his feet. "Well, I best be hitting the trail."

"Is there anything I can do to assist you?"

"Just wish me luck. I've got some snake hunting to do."

Basil's Journal: Wednesday, January 5th

I may be making the worst mistake of my life.

I've decided not to tell Griffin about my conversation with Sukalli yesterday evening. Sukalli disagrees with me, but promises to keep quiet for now.

Until we know more, I do not see how knowing all this could be anything but a burden to Fin.

Chapter Four

"Like I'm *so* going to diagram sentences as an adult," Katie Heflin said under her breath. She marked the final line on the worksheet, shoved it into a folder, then hopped up from her desk. After several minutes of rummaging in her closet for her jacket, she spied it on her bed, half buried under a mountain of clothes. She yanked it loose in an avalanche of tees and jeans and headed downstairs to the front door.

"Mom," she yelled, hopping on one foot as she pulled on her Uggs. "I'm going across the street to Griffin's."

"Come here a minute," Helen Heflin called from the living room over the rustle of newspaper. "It's important."

Uh-oh, that doesn't sound good, Katie thought. She tucked her jacket under one arm as she headed into the room, mentally reviewing for any misdemeanors. *Nope, all clear.* She walked over and perched on the arm of the sofa next to her mother. "Yeah?"

Helen started to speak, then paused. "Is that my sweater?"

Katie looked down at the snug-fitting black turtleneck. "Yup. But you got to admit, it looks better on me." She changed the subject. "So what's up?"

"I spoke with Basil today," Helen said, her eyes the same blue-green as her daughter's. "He'd really like Griffin to start school. He thinks it might help him adjust, but he's having a hard time convincing him. I guess the boy's not too thrilled with the idea."

"That's for sure. I tried to talk to him about it last week, but he just shut me down. He's changed, Mom, and not just the angel to mortal thing." She snorted and glanced down at her mother. "My boyfriend, who used to be an angel." They both smiled regretfully for a moment. "It's like he's mad. All the time. At everybody."

"Well, he is. Being a Terrae Angelus was how he defined himself. So right now he's confused and angry. And he doesn't see a place for himself in this world. Try to encourage him to at least *think* about going to school. But be patient with him. Let him know that being mortal doesn't change how you feel about him. Okay?"

"It doesn't change how I feel—that's what I keep telling him. Over and over. And it'd be great if we were in school together. But I'm afraid if I mention it again, he's going to think I'm secretly happy he's human now." She rubbed her palms along her jeans. "I don't want to make him feel any worse."

"I don't think that possible." Helen patted her daughter's knee. "You better go. Be back by six."

Katie gave a nod and left. She hurried across the street, her nose stinging from the frigid air, and trotted up the steps. As she raised her hand to knock, the door swung open.

"Why, hello, miss." Basil smiled as he ushered her inside. "Good day at school?" He took her jacket and hung it up as she toed off her boots.

"Yeah, thanks, Mr. Raine." She nudged her footwear under the bench. Tucking her pale hair behind one ear, she lowered her voice. "How's he doing today?"

"About the same. By any chance, did your mother speak with you?" he asked, studying her face.

She nodded.

"Right. So would you be willing to prod him a bit about attending school?"

"Well, I'll try. Just hope it doesn't cause another explosion. If you know what I mean."

"I'm still removing shrapnel from last one," he replied with a trace of a wink, then waved his hand. "Fin's in the kitchen. Why don't you go on back and surprise him."

As Basil returned to his study, Katie padded down the hall in her socks. A smile spread across her face; speeding up, she rounded the archway.

And barreled into Griffin rushing from the kitchen.

"Oh!" she squealed as she bounced off of him. She staggered backwards, her feet skidding on the wood floor.

"Katie!" Unable to slow his momentum, Griffin flung his arms around her as they toppled over. For a long minute, time seemed to stand still. Then, cradling Katie against his chest, he spun in midair. He landed on his back with a grunt, cushioning her fall with his body.

Stunned, they laid there, staring wide-eyed at each other with their faces inches away.

"Wow," she breathed after a moment. "How did you do that? It was just like when you saved me from that car."

"I have no idea," he whispered back.

She smiled. "Well, I'm glad you did."

"Ahem." They looked up at Basil standing in the doorway. "Do I want to know?" he asked.

"We ran into each other," they said simultaneously and laughed. Katie hopped up, her face red. Griffin rubbed his elbow as he clambered to his feet.

"Good thing she landed on you," Basil said, nodding from one to the other, "Instead of vice versa."

"You should have seen it, Mr. Raine. He flipped around so that I wouldn't hit the floor. He took the fall for me." She squeezed Griffin's hand as she held on to it with both of hers.

"Always the knight in shining armor, eh, Fin?"

"Yeah, right. Come on, Katie." He tugged her toward the living room as Basil headed upstairs.

Griffin's Fire

Hand in hand, they flopped down on the sofa. Griffin punched the remote to lower the volume on the blaring television. Propping his feet on the coffee table, he draped an arm around Katie as she snuggled against his side, resting her hand on his thigh. He placed his other hand on top of hers, splaying her fingers apart with his own.

"I missed you today," he murmured. "It sucks that you're back in school—I got used to having you around all the time during winter break."

"Missed you more."

"So did you give your report?"

"Nah. The teacher was absent, so we had a sub. I'm doing it tomorrow." Katie bit her lip. "Um…Griffin? About school…" She froze, feeling the sudden tension in his body.

"What about it?"

"I know we've talked about it before, but—"

"I told you already. Not my thing."

"I know. But maybe you could just think about it? I mean, we'd be together. At least part of the day. It'd be fun."

"Yeah, until I do something stupid."

"Griffin, you know more stuff than most of the teachers. And I'll be there, and you already know Carlee—" Katie stopped when he yanked his arm free.

He twisted around to look her full in the face. "Listen," he said through gritted teeth. "I don't want to go. So drop it. Okay?" Glancing away, he muttered under his breath. "Fire, get a clue."

Katie's cheeks reddened. She looked down, took a deep breath, and then raised her chin. "I'm not going to get in another fight with you. I just feel—"

"Sorry for me? Is that what you feel?"

"No, that's not what I'm—"

"Because I don't want it and I don't need it."

"Well, excuse me for caring about you."

Darby Karchut

"Hey, I didn't ask for your pity." He jumped up and stomped over to the fireplace, his hands fisted at his sides. He glanced at the flames snapping and cracking around the logs, then closed his eyes. "Was that the only reason you came over? To nag me about school?"

"No—I wanted to see you. Unless you're going to be in a pissy mood again." She stood up and glared at his back. "Maybe I should just take off," she said after a few moments.

"Fine. Go."

Katie blinked back sudden tears, then whirled around and left. The front door closed with a thud.

Griffin banged his fist against his leg in frustration. *Why won't everyone just leave me alone? Stop bugging me about school. Like that's going to solve everything.* He propped an elbow on the mantel and traced the thin pale scar bisecting his right eyebrow, trying to ignore the Voice.

Katie's just trying to help, you moron. Help you fit in to your new life. But of course, you had to be a jerk to her. Typical.

With a growl, Griffin spun around, darted across the room to the hall, and yanked the door open. Bolting down the steps, he hollered at the slender figure running away. "Katie. Katie, wait." His breath puffed around him as he chased after her.

Halfway across the snow-packed street, he slipped and crashed to one knee. Wincing, he looked up just as her door slammed shut. "Smooth move," he muttered to himself, and then clambered to his feet. He rubbed his leg as he gazed at her house. His heart swelled with hope when her bedroom lights flicked on, then sank when the window blinds rolled down.

He turned around. Dread shot through his body like an arctic blast of wind. "Oh, great."

Basil stood in the open doorway.

Their eyes met. Then the Mentor pointed at a spot in front of him with an angry stab of his finger.

Griffin's Fire

He's going to rip me apart, Griffin thought as he trudged home, *for being rude to a guest, who also a friend, who happens to be a girl. Wow. A trifecta.* He squared his shoulders and climbed the porch. Shivering in his tee shirt from more than just the cold, he stopped in front of Basil and took a deep breath.

"Look, I already know what you're going to say. 'That was incredibly boorish behavior, Griffin. You must never be rude like that. And especially never to a young lady,'" he said, mimicking Basil's English accent. "I'm sorry, but I just got mad. I tried to apologize to her, but she was too pissed off. And I don't blame her. Because I acted like a real you-know-what." He tucked his arms closer to his body and shivered again. "Don't worry. I'll go over tomorrow and beg for forgiveness, okay? So can I…I mean, *may I* come inside now or do I have to spend the night huddled on the door mat?"

"Do not tempt me." Basil glared down at him for a while longer, watching as Griffin shifted from foot to foot. Finally, he cuffed him lightly on the head and shooed him inside. "You delivered a first-rate lecture, though. One of mine, I take it?"

Griffin nodded as he slipped off his shoes in the entryway. Kicking them to one side, he slumped on the bench. Basil joined him. For a few minutes, they sat in silence, watching the snowy tracks melt on the tile floor.

"Basil?"

"Fin."

"Do you think…" He stopped and cleared his throat. "Do you think maybe someday…I mean, is there any chance I could change back? Back into a Terrae Angelus?"

"No, lad."

"I didn't think so." He glanced sideways. "I keep pretending that this will all go away. You know? Like Command will realize Nicopolis is a crazy psycho and it was a mistake and fix me somehow.

Darby Karchut

Or I'd wake up and this would be just one of those gosh-awful nightmares I have." He curled forward, resting his elbows on his knees, his head hanging down. "Basil, what's wrong with me? Why does all of this horrible crap keep happening to me?"

Basil butted Griffin with his shoulder. "Listen and listen well. There is nothing wrong with you. You are *Griffin*, and that's a wondrous thing to be."

"Oh, yeah? And just who is Griffin?" he asked, still looking down.

Basil smiled as he leaned over and whispered, "Whomever he chooses."

Chapter Five

Katie's Journal: Thursday, January 6th
Another fight yesterday!
We fight and make up. We fight and make up. Sometimes, we just fight. I hate having a boyfriend. Who used to be an angel. Who's now a human.
Sounds like a really lame book. Or a bad movie.
I want the old Griffin back. The one with the smile that could light up the city. The one that gave me my first real kiss. The Griffin that saved my dog. Saved my family. Saved me.
I don't like this new Griffin. And I don't like feeling this way about him.

Griffin's Journal: Thursday, January 6th
What a rotten week already. I mouthed off to Basil. I got in another argument with Katie. I tried to pick a fight with Katie's dog, but he just ran around like an idiot, trying to get me to play. Stupid Bear.
I feel like I'm standing by a dark hole and I keep looking down into it. And I just know if I inch any closer, I'll slid in. But I can't seem to step back. I can't seem to move at all.
Maybe the universe won't notice me if I stay perfectly still. And maybe it'll stop kicking me in the butt.

***

Griffin flinched as the cane whistled through the air. Curled in a tight ball on the concrete floor of the basement, the ten-year-old covered his head with his arms, trying to protect his face. He bit his lip, determined not to cry aloud as a second blow burned across his legs, raising another welt.

"What will it take for you to follow simple directions?" Nicopolis snarled. "Is this how it is going to be for the rest of your apprenticeship? In all my years, I've never had a Tiro as incompetent as you, you filthy little Earth and Fire." The Mentor swept his lank hair to one side and took a deep breath. "Now that I have your full attention, perhaps you can explain why you failed to stop the second bus."

"I'm sorry, Mentor," Griffin said, his voice muffled by his arms. "I...I tried. But you said use Might and mine wasn't strong enough, so I thought maybe if I—" He froze and squeezed his eyes tight as Nicopolis raised his arm. The cane's shadow weaved like a cobra in the gloom of the single light bulb.

"Are you blaming me *for your poor performance?"*

"No, Mentor. It's just I can't—"

"Quiet!" Nicopolis toed Griffin in the side. "Get up. I'm weary of speaking to a cowering lump."

Griffin scrambled to his feet. He winced as his pants rubbed against the welts on his legs. Fixing his eyes on a crack in the floor, he knotted his fingers along the legs of his too-large jeans to keep his hands from shaking.

"When Command assigned you to me, I knew it was a mistake," Nicopolis said, his pale eyes unblinking. "And these last few months have proven me correct." He tapped the handle of the cane against Griffin's chest in rhythm with his words. "If I do not see a vast *improvement, life is going to become much more unpleasant for you. Do you understand?" Griffin nodded with frantic jerks of his head. Nicopolis stepped back and glanced around the spotless basement, adjusting his tie. "This place is a pig sty. If you want to eat today, I suggest you start cleaning."*

"Yes, Mentor," Griffin whispered. He dragged the back of his hand down his tear-stained face, leaving smears across his cheeks. Turning around, he headed for the broom closet, dread chilling his spine like it always did whenever

he turned his back on Nicopolis. Quickening his pace, he stumbled and tripped over his own feet. Sweat broke out on his forehead as he fell.

Griffin rolled off his bed and hit the carpet with a thud, quilt and sheets tangled around his legs. Panting, he kicked free as he scanned the empty shadows of his bedroom, Nicopolis' voice still hissing at him from the nightmare.

"Oh, God, I'm getting sick of this," he moaned. He pulled his knees up and rested his forehead against them; his damp tee shirt clung to his body. His pulse thundered in his ears. Closing his eyes, he drew in a deep breath through his nose and let it out through his mouth as he waited for his heart to slow.

A hand grabbed his shoulder.

With a strangled cry, Griffin fell backwards. He swung his fist at the dark shape looming over him. A solid grip caught his wrist in midair.

"Steady, lad." Basil released the boy's arm and crouched down. "It's just me," he said, his voice an anchor. "Another bad dream, eh?"

"Yeah."

"Do you wish to tell me about this one?"

Griffin shook his head. He clenched his jaw as he fought the nausea rising in his throat.

"Are you certain? It might help if you—"

Before Basil could finish, Griffin scrambled to his feet, nearly tripping over the pile of quilt and sheets. He bolted through the door of the adjacent bathroom and skidded to his knees in front of the toilet. Cold sweat broke out along his back as he vomited. He heaved again, spasms racking his stomach.

Worry clouded Basil's face. He rose and made his way over to the doorway. He flicked on the lights and grimaced at the sour smell.

After gagging once more with nothing coming up but bile, Griffin slumped back on the floor. He wiped his watering eyes with the

Darby Karchut

hem of his shirt, his face pale except for the greenish tinge around his lips. "Just something I ate."

"I've heard that before," Basil said. He reached over and flushed the toilet, then filled a drinking glass with water and handed it to Griffin.

As Griffin rinsed and spat, Basil plucked a washcloth from the counter and dampened it with cold water. "Here. Clean your face." Leaning against the sink, he studied Griffin and shook his head at the dark circles under the teen's eyes. "Fin, we really should talk about—" He paused as a shaft of Light shot across the bedroom.

As the voice spoke from within the beam, Griffin tightened his hand around the glass. *This one sounds rough*, he thought. *I wish I was going with him.* He looked up as Basil sighed.

"On my way," he acknowledged, and then peered at Griffin still kneeling on the floor. "Duty calls. Will you be all right?"

Griffin rose and took a seat on the edge of the bathtub. "I'm good. And don't worry about me. That's how you get hurt on missions—by not paying attention." His grin faded when he noticed Basil staring thoughtfully at him.

"It's still my place to worry about you."

"Yeah. Well. Not tonight, okay?"

Basil smiled and clapped him on the shoulder. "I'll check in when I return."

A gust ruffled Griffin's hair as Basil disappeared, the breeze cooling his forehead. "Be careful, Mentor," he muttered to the empty room, the scent of rain on the wind lingering.

Griffin's Journal: Friday, January 7th

I don't think I'll be going back to sleep for awhile. That was one heck of a nightmare. The kind that makes me worship at the porcelain throne.

Sometimes, I can't believe it's been three years since Basil rescued me and took me on as his Tiro. Man, I loved working with him. I learned so much, even though he's a Wind and Water and I'm an Earth and Fire.

I mean, I used to be.

We had even talked a few times about teaming up after my apprenticeship was over. Our combined Elements would have made us unstoppable. Lots of Terrae Angeli work in teams—it's safer that way. Too many Terrae Angeli die in the field.

Now that I think about it, he taught me a lot more than just how to be a guardian angel.

So maybe it's time.

Time to face up to the fact that I'm human.

And start using *his* lessons in *this* life.

Katie's Journal: Friday, January 7th

I can't sleep. Keep thinking about him. I just noticed his bedroom lights are on, too.

I came to a decision tonight. I'm going to do whatever I can to help him. Not because I think I can do much. But because that's what friends do.

That's what he would do.

Chapter Six

Dawn edged sideways through the half closed drapes and cast a bar of light across Griffin's face. He rolled over and burrowed into his pillow, kicking a foot out from under the quilt.

Something smacked against the window, rattling the glass. He jerked awake. *What the heck was that?* He lifted his head, his face creased with sleep. At the second thump, he flung the covers aside, lurched off his bed, and staggered to the window. Opening the drapes wider, he peered out, squinting from the first rays of the sun reflecting off the snow. He glanced down into the yard. "Oops!" He ducked behind one of the panels as he gave his boxers a tug.

Katie stood in the driveway dressed in sweats. She cocked her arm back, her hand loaded with another snowball, and eyeballed his window. Spying him, she paused and waved.

Griffin glanced over his shoulder at his tee shirt on the floor next to his bed. He shrugged, and then pushed up the window. Its wooden frame creaked from the cold. He squatted down and leaned out; he stifled a yelp when his bare chest made contact with the snow on the sill. "What's going on?"

"I came to see if you wanted to run with me this morning," she called up to him, bouncing up and down on her toes, her face and nose pink. "Decide quick, because I'm freezing my butt off."

And I wouldn't want that *to happen*, he thought. "Be right down." He shut the window and dressed hastily, then tiptoed down the stairs and headed to the kitchen. After leaving a note for Basil by the coffee maker, he tugged on his cap and gloves and slipped out the front door.

Griffin jogged across the lawn covered in an icing of snow. He broke into a sprint as he neared Katie. With a whoop, he flung his arms around her and lifted her off her feet. She shrieked as he spun around, her hat flying off.

"Hey, put me down."

"Not until I get a kiss."

"A kiss? No way."

"Why, I brushed my teeth."

"Nah, still too high a price. I'll just stay here." They both laughed, then he lowered her to the ground and hugged her.

"What a great way to wake up," Griffin whispered in her ear.

"Yeah," Katie said. "Too bad we can only really hang out on the weekends."

Not if we were in school together, Griffin thought. Startled, he pulled back and blinked. *Now where did that come from?*

"Something wrong?"

"Uh…no. It's all good. Come on, let's get moving before I have to defrost you." He reached down and snatched her fleece hat out of the snow, slapping it against his leg before handing it to her.

They jogged side-by-side along the street. Their breaths smoked out behind them as they settled into a steady pace. Colorado's famous champagne powder swirled around their ankles in miniature flurries. Another dawn greeter ran toward them on the opposite side of the street. A Labrador trotted at her heel. Its black pelt was silver-tipped with frost.

Out of habit, Griffin braced himself. The owner and dog drew nearer. The dog glanced briefly at Griffin, and then swung its head to stare down a crow screeching from a nearby tree. The woman gave a wave as she and her pet passed and continued along the street. Their tracks left twin furrows in the snow.

"Well, I guess I won't have to worry about dogs going insane around me anymore," Griffin joked with a grin. His smile never reached his eyes. In mid-stride, Katie took his hand and gave it a squeeze.

They left the residential area and headed toward High Springs' downtown. A snowplow clanked and rumbled past. As they slowed to avoid the spray of snow from its blade, Griffin gazed at the sun coloring the western mountains in a wash of purples. *I wonder how many times Basil hauled me outside to watch the sunrise? Or view the stars? Or check out a hawk perched on the back fence?* "Angel or mortal, Fin, you must agree it's a beautiful world, eh?" Griffin could hear his Mentor's voice. *He's right about that. Of course, he's right about a lot of things. So maybe he's right about school. Probably time I start dealing with all this.*

"Hey," he panted. "Let's run over to Centennial. Make a loop around the campus."

Katie peeked out of the corner of her eye. "Okay, I'll bite. Why?"

He slowed to a walk, then stopped to catch his breath. As she jogged in place beside him, he pulled off his cap and twirled it around on his finger. Steam rose from his sweat soaked hair. "I just wanted to see where all the buildings are. You know. To get a feel for…" He trailed off at her expression. "Look! Before you start going all squealy—"

"I do not squeal."

"Katie, you're a girl. You *so* squeal. Whenever you're excited about *anything*." Ignoring her protests, he continued, "I'm not committing. Just thinking about it. Okay?"

"No commitment. Just thinking," she acknowledged. "Got it." She grinned ear to ear.

Then squealed.

* * *

Griffin's Fire

"I beg your pardon?" Basil stood frozen in the middle of the kitchen, his coffee mug halfway to his mouth.

"I said, maybe you and Miss Lena were right. Maybe I should go to school." Griffin sat down at the table and toed off his running shoes. "Guess it's time I start adjusting." He wiped his damp face on his sleeve.

"Are you certain about this?"

"No, not really. But I need to do something. Right? Find a way to live this life. Otherwise, Nicopolis wins."

Basil walked over and joined him. "What changed your mind?"

Griffin pulled his leg up and planted his foot on the chair. "Do you remember that night? A few months after I became your apprentice? When we stayed up late talking and I told you *everything*? How bad it was when Nicopolis was my Mentor?" Basil nodded. "Well, you said I had a choice. I could let what happened to me box me in. Or I could step out of that box and be who I was meant to be." Griffin rested his chin on his upright knee. "I guess this is the same thing. I can't be a Terrae Angelus…" He paused and cleared his throat. "So I better start figuring out how to climb out of *this* box. And learn how to be a human."

"It'll be a new world for you, Fin. It might be more of a challenge than either of us realize. Your education as a Tiro didn't exactly parallel mortals, to say the least. Not unless they offer Might use and manipulating the Elements as subjects."

Griffin nodded. "Do you know what I miss most about being a Terrae Angelus? I mean, besides helping people? I miss controlling Earth and Fire. Especially Fire."

"And how are you feeling? Now that you've had time to adjust?"

"A lot better. Not so tired anymore. You were right about it taking awhile to get used to the additional load. Do humans realize just how much their mortality actually weighs?" Griffin shook his head. "Remember last week? I could barely walk up the stairs."

"I remember," Basil said as he stared into his mug, swirling his coffee. He started to speak, and then changed the subject. "Best go take your shower. I'll start breakfast." When Griffin left the kitchen, Basil sat for a minute. He stood and tightened the belt around his robe, then snatched the phone off the wall, punching the speed dial.

"Good morning, Lena. Did I wake—No, no, nothing's wrong. In fact, I have some good news for a change. Would the Foundation be able to help with the necessary paperwork to get Griffin enrolled in school on Monday? Yes, school." He laughed at her hoot of delight. "Marvelous. We'll see you this afternoon."

* * *

"Why, this is incredible, Lena. How in Heaven's name did you manage to pull this together in one day?" Basil sat at his desk and flipped through the file folder, scanning page after page. Griffin stood behind him, peering over his shoulder.

"It's what I do," Lena said. "I *am* your human liaison with the Foundation, after all. And if our organization can't handle this level of documentation, then we don't deserve our reputation."

Griffin pulled out a paper and squinted at it. "When did I test for advanced history classes?"

Lena snapped her fingers. "Quick. How long has the Foundation existed in North America?" she fired at him.

"Um...middle of the sixteen hundreds. But what does that have to do with—"

"Next question. Explain the primary role of the Foundation."

"Well, it's an underground organization made up of humans who help Terrae Angeli with paperwork, money, houses, and other stuff so we can fit in with modern society while keeping our real identities hidden. That way we're more effective in helping people," Griffin said, a frown of confusion on his face. "But I don't think they teach about the Foundation in public high school. You know, since it's supposed to be a *secret* and all."

"Don't be pert. Now, final question. What was High Springs' nickname during its early years and why?"

"*Little London*, because of the number of British tourists who visited here in the late nineteenth century. Some even stayed permanently."

"And not just British tourists," Basil said, enjoying the exchange. He took the paper from Griffin and placed it back in the file. "Right, Fin. I believe you just took the history test." He gestured toward the sofa. "Now go sit—you're hovering."

Lena smiled as Griffin flopped down next to her. She patted his hand. "I'm very proud of you, *liebling*, making this decision."

"Just hope I don't screw up too bad."

"Badly. You hope you don't screw up too *badly*," Basil corrected, still absorbed in the papers before him.

Whatever, Griffin mouthed.

Lena checked her watch. "I must go. I'm attending a fundraiser for the Fine Arts Center tonight. Basil, you'll let me know if you need anything else, yes?"

"I certainly will. Fin, please escort Lena to her car, that's a good lad."

Lena leaned over and whispered something to Griffin. He laughed as she stood up.

"You got that right, Miss Lena."

"I'll teach you that expression in German next time."

"Do I even want to know?" Basil asked. Griffin and Lena grinned at each other. "Most likely not," he decided.

"*Auf Wiedersehen*, you two." With a nod, Lena headed down the hall and out the front door.

Griffin waved a goodbye at her through the window. He yawned and stretched out on the sofa.

"Basil?"

"Fin."

Darby Karchut

"Are we going with our usual cover story?" He shoved a pillow under his head and closed his eyes. "You know. Father and son. You teaching me at home and all that?"

"I believe so. We're familiar with it and it does parallel the information in this file." Basil dug out a pen from the desk drawer. "But be aware that many people have negative opinions about home schooling. You might experience criticism from other students and even some teachers." He shook his head at the drowsy grunt.

As Griffin dozed, Basil signed several more pages, the scratching of his pen a soothing whisper in the peaceful room. He closed the file and rocked back in his chair. A corner of his mouth twitched. Pointing his hand like a gun, he took careful aim. An icy spray squirted from the tip of his finger and nailed Griffin in the face.

"Hey!" Griffin sputtered as he jerked upright. He wiped his face. "That's it—payback time," he announced, his brown eyes dancing. He flung out his hand toward Basil, palm forward.

Nothing happened.

Griffin lowered his arm, his grin fading.

"Oh, Fin, my apologies. I did not mean to remind you—"

"Nah, it's okay. No harm, no foul." He checked his watch. "I think I'll go call Katie. Let her know what's going on about school." Before Basil could speak, he pushed off the sofa and left.

Basil's Journal: Saturday, January 8th

What we would do without Lena Weiss is beyond me. She is the most resourceful human I've every known, and certainly one of the kindest. Griffin loves her like an aunt. And I'm honored to have her as a friend.

Sukalli contacted me a few days ago. Still no luck, but if anyone can find Nicopolis and bring him in for questioning, it will be the Guardian. His skill as a hunter and warrior is unequal in this day and age.

Griffin has decided to try attending school. Certainly he will be the proverbial stranger in a strange land. But if he can handle public high school, then I believe he will be able to handle anything life throws at him.

Chapter Seven

"Mr. Raine? I'm James Navarre, the sophomore counselor." The trim, hawk-faced man straightened his tie as he walked into the office. Most of its small space was occupied by a row of metal filing cabinets and a paper-strewn desk. "I'm sorry to keep you waiting. Mondays, you know."

"Not a problem—thank you for seeing us this morning on such short notice." Basil stood up. He shook hands with and handed the file folder to the man. "This is my son, Griffin."

"Sir." Griffin stuck out his hand.

As Navarre clasped it, he raised his eyebrows, his dark eyes curious. "Let me take a guess—your dad's military?" he asked as he leaned over the desk and picked up his ringing telephone.

"Retired—British Intelligence," Griffin said with a trace of resignation. *Why did he have to pick that as part of our cover story? Sounds goofier every time I say it.* As the counselor answered the phone, Basil nudged him with his elbow and hummed the James Bond theme under his breath. Griffin rolled his eyes.

"...and hold my calls, please." Hanging up, Navarre gestured for them to resume their seats, then perched on the corner of his desk and opened the file, taking a moment to search through it. "Looks like we might also need health records...oh, wait. Here they are." He walked around and settled in front of his computer. "Give me a few minutes to come up with a schedule, Griffin. Since the semester's already begun, you might not get first choice of your classes." He tapped away as he checked various papers.

While they waited, Griffin spotted a framed photograph on the counselor's desk. A plump, but elegant dark-haired woman posed seated in the center, holding a little girl in a yellow dress on her lap while a teenage boy and Mr. Navarre stood behind.

"Your family, I take it?" Basil asked, also noticing the photo.

"My pride and joy. Tessie is our three year old terror. And Cas is a sophomore here at Centennial to his everlasting mortification. According to him, nothing is worse than El Papá being around all day." He finished typing and hit the print button. As the printer began swooshing out papers, he smiled at Griffin. "Do you have any brothers or sisters?"

"No, sir. It's just Dad and me."

"Do you know any one here at Centennial?"

"My girlfriend, Katie Heflin. Oh, and Carlee Webb. And I've run into a junior, Nash Baylor, a few times." *And took him on in a fight along with three of his friends just last month*, he thought to himself. *Probably shouldn't mention* that *my first day.*

"Okay, Griffin, here's your schedule, locker assignment, student handbook, and a map of the campus," Navarre said, pulling the sheets out of the tray. The bell rang, drowning him out for a moment. Shouts and laughter and slamming lockers reverberated through the halls. He raised his voice as he continued. "Sophomores are not allowed off campus for lunch, so you might—" He halted at the rap on his partially open door.

"Hey, Dad? Are you busy…oh, sorry." A lanky boy began backing out until Navarre waved him in.

"Cas, I want you to meet a new student who's starting tomorrow." The boy sauntered in and stood next to his father. "This is Griffin Raine and his dad."

"Hi, Mr. Raine. Hey, Griffin," Cas said, a younger version of his father, with the same black hair and warm, cinnamon skin. "Know your schedule yet?" Griffin nodded and held it out for the other

Darby Karchut

boy. Cas scanned it. "Awesome—you're in my AP history class. Now I won't be the only brilliant sophomore in there."

"Bragging?" asked his father.

"It's not bragging when it's the truth," he replied with a crooked grin.

Navarre snorted and changed the subject. "Son, why did you come by?"

"Oh. I need money for lunch. I forgot to get some from Mom this morning."

Basil and Navarre exchanged amused glances. The counselor reached into his back pocket and pulled out a wallet.

"I suppose it'd be considered child abuse to let you go hungry." Handing some bills over, he glanced at the wall clock. "Don't you have a class in a few minutes?"

"Just study hall." Cas tucked the money into his pocket. "Thanks, Dad. I better go."

"Wait a sec. I have a job for you." Navarre cocked his head toward Griffin. "Give him a quick tour of campus. I'll let your teacher know where you are." He shooed the two boys out of his office.

"Sorry about this," Griffin said, struggling to keep up with Cas as the crowd battered him from side to side. *It's like whitewater rafting*, he thought. *Without the raft*. He glanced around, trying to memorize the layout while scanning for Katie. "I've got a map if you need to go do something else."

After scooting around a corner, Cas paused and waited. "Are you kidding? Anything to get out of study hall." Squeezing past a knot of teachers blocking traffic, Cas led the way down a corridor lined on one side with floor to ceiling windows framing High Springs' famous peak.

"Where did you go to school before?" Cas asked as they headed across campus to the academic wing. The mob thinned as the next period began.

"Home schooled." Griffin tightened his lips and steeled himself.

"Lucky. Must be nice to concentrate on stuff you're really interested in and skip the boring subjects."

Griffin nodded, relaxing. "Yeah, it was. I'm going to miss working with my dad," he said without thinking. He winced. "Okay—that was lame."

"Pretty much." Cas grinned, taking the sting out of the comment.

Griffin grinned back.

With Cas pointing out landmarks and shortcuts, they located most of Griffin's classes along with his locker. They finished up outside of the cafeteria as the next bell rang.

"That's second lunch so I need to go eat. Know the way back?"

"No problem." Griffin checked his map as he shoved his schedule into his back pocket, then looked at the other boy. "Thanks for helping me out. Sorry if I screwed up your morning."

"It's all good. See you in history tomorrow." Cas turned and jostled into line while Griffin headed toward the front of the school.

Fighting his way back through the teeming hall, he winced at the cacophony of noise assaulting him—lockers crashing shut and voices strident with emotions, either excitement or frustration. Or anger.

He jumped when a hand seized his elbow. Whirling around, he found himself face to face with Katie. His heart skipped a beat at her smile.

"When did you get here?" she asked, pulling him to one side of the crowd.

"About an hour ago. I just finished a tour. Want to see my schedule?" He dug it out and handed it to her, then leaned against a locker.

She scanned it. "Yes! We have the same lunch. I was so hoping." She examined the rest of it. "Oh, no—you got Milton for math."

"Is that bad?"

"Totally. The guy's pure evil. But hey—we got study hall together second period." She leaned closer and slipped her arms around his waist. "So welcome to Centennial, Griffin Raine."

"Are you this friendly with all the new students?"

"Nah—just the good-looking ones. Boys, I mean," she added quickly. "Good looking *boys*."

"You had me worried there for a minute," he joked as he squeezed her back. He froze when someone cleared their throat. Looking up, he saw a bespectacled girl loaded with books.

"Why don't you two get a room so I can open my locker?"

Get a room? Griffin mouthed.

Katie blushed, then grabbed his hand and led him away toward the cafeteria. "I've got lunch now. You want to come eat with me?"

"Yeah, that'd be great…oh, no." Griffin stopped. "Basil's waiting for me back at the office. I better go."

"Oh," she said, disappointed. "Well, let me walk you over. I still have some time."

Strolling hand in hand, Katie frowned at the looks from other girls when they spotted Griffin. When two senior girls turned and whistled at him, he looked back in bewilderment.

"What was *that* about?"

"Cougars," Katie muttered under her breath. "I'll explain later."

Griffin's Journal: Monday, January 10th

I can't believe I'm starting high school tomorrow. Still doesn't seem real. I've got lunch and study hall with Katie, but no classes.

Better memorize the map so I don't have to keep looking at it like some moron.

Basil's Journal: Monday, January 10th

I took Fin over to Centennial High and registered him for school this morning. We celebrated afterwards with lunch at Wooglin's Deli downtown. Unfortunately, the lad had a severe migraine attack during the meal. He quite lost his appetite after only a few bites of his pastrami sandwich.

Odd.

He rarely gets headaches.

Chapter Eight

Helen Heflin kneed the refrigerator door closed, a head of lettuce in each hand. She dumped them in the sink and began tearing the leaves apart as she rinsed. "I said no."

"But, Mom," Katie tried again from the corner of the kitchen. "Mr. Raine said any time I want to bring him with us, I can."

"No."

"But I've haven't seen him all day. Except for like five seconds."

"Still no."

"He won't bother anyone. I promise."

"Oh, sure. Until he knocks something over. Or pees on the floor." Helen shook the lettuce dry and tossed it in a large bowl, adding chopped vegetables and olive oil.

"Please tell me you're discussing your dog and not your boyfriend," Lewis Heflin said, his head buried in the pantry closet as he rummaged about. "Helen, I cannot find the wine anywhere. Are you sure you said on the right hand side?"

"I said in the refrigerator, dear." She shook her head. "Absentminded professor," she murmured under her breath.

He straightened up, just missing the shelf with his head. "Oh. Well. That would explain it. What time does Basil expect us?"

Helen dried her hands, then snapped a lid on the bowl. "Ten minutes ago, so let's move it, people. Lewis, take the wine. Katie, the pie."

"So can I bring Bear?" She begged one more time. "Please?"

Helen stopped, a finger raised in warning. "You promise to keep a close eye on him? Every minute?"

Katie nodded and spun around before her mother could change her mind, opening the dog kennel with a metallic clang. "C'mon, big guy," she said as she snapped the leash on Bear's collar. She smoothed the gray-brown tufts sprouting over his eyes. "Want to go see Griffin?" The enormous wolfhound whined and thumped his tail at the mention of Griffin's name. Katie grabbed the pie with her free hand and headed down the hall to the front door, Bear trotting beside her. Lewis and Helen trailed behind.

As they reached Basil's front porch, Bear strained on his leash. When Griffin opened the door, the dog lunged for him, almost jerking Katie off her feet.

"I got him," Griffin said, grabbing the lead. "Hey, Bear." He stroked the giant's neck, then ran a hand down his side and thumped his ribs. "You just wanted some attention, didn't you?" The wolfhound panted blissfully, gazing up in adoration.

"The loyalty of a dog is boundless," Lewis remarked. "And anytime you want him, young man, I'll be happy to sell...no, *give* him to you."

"Hey, quit trying to get rid of my baby." Katie grinned at the old family joke.

Lewis smiled and ushered his wife and daughter inside. Pausing to lay a hand on Griffin's shoulder, he gave it a squeeze. "How are you holding up?" he asked in an undertone, lingering in the hall while Helen and Katie made their way back to the kitchen. Bear sat between them, pressed against Griffin's leg.

"Okay, I think." He reached down to ruffle the dog's ears. "Ask me tomorrow after my first day. Katie says I've got a cruel algebra teacher and a tough social studies class."

"Well, thanks to your unique upbringing, you've a strong background in world events. I'm sure you won't have any problems in

Darby Karchut

history, not with Basil around to assist you." The professor cleared his throat. "Speaking of which, there's a question I've always wanted to ask. Please tell me if you're not allowed to answer it."

"Uh…sure."

"Just how old *is* Basil?"

"You mean in earth years? Well, I can tell you this much. We…I mean, Terrae Angeli…age at a different rate than humans. The older they get, the slower they age."

"That would make Basil…"

"Let's just say that he was a Tiro when the Kellsfarne manuscript was still a rough draft."

"Holy cow!"

* * *

"So what are you wearing tomorrow?" Katie asked Griffin as she took another bite of artichoke lasagna. At the other end of the table, Basil and Helen listened with amusement at Lewis' misadventure with his new cell phone during his lecture on world religions.

"Clothes. Otherwise, it would be an awkward first day." He grinned and patted her on the back when she choked with laughter. He looked up when Basil stopped talking.

"Griffin!"

"What? I didn't do anything. She's the one—"

"If you two are finished, you may leave the table. Before I'm required to perform the Heimlich maneuver."

Katie took a sip of water and wiped her eyes. "Let's go up and look at your stuff. I'll help you pick something out."

"Whoopee," Griffin mumbled under his breath. "Aren't I supposed to clean up?" He looked hopefully at Basil.

A wicked grin spread across the Mentor's face. "Why, Fin, I wouldn't dream of interrupting your sartorial endeavors. In fact,

Katie, would you select his outfits for the entire week? Thank you, miss." He waved a hand in dismissal.

"And take Bear with you," Helen added. The dog jumped up from the corner at the sound of his name. His tail beat out a joyful rhythm.

They headed through the house and up the stairs, Bear in the lead, and Griffin on Katie's heels. Halfway, he reached out and snagged her ankle.

Katie giggled as she stumbled. "Hey, knock it off." Sprinting the rest of the way, she darted ahead into his bedroom and turned around, holding her breath.

She squealed when Griffin dashed through the doorway and tackled her, flinging her onto the bed. Bear followed and sat down nearby with a yawn, scratching behind one ear.

"You're dead meat, Heflin." Griffin pinned her down and tickled her, ignoring her breathless protests. "I'll help you pick out an outfit," he said in a falsetto voice, then yelped when her knee jerked upward and smacked into his thigh. "Hey—watch your aim." He renewed his attack.

"Okay, okay," Katie shrieked. "You can go to school naked—I don't care. Just stop. Please."

He paused and gazed down at her. "Promise?"

Panting, she blew a strand of hair out of her eyes. "Promise what?"

"That I can go to school naked?"

"Yeah—like you would." She wiggled free and headed over to the closet, nudging Bear to one side. "Move over, you horse. Go. Park it." She pointed to the far corner. The dog hesitated, then sauntered over and flopped down.

Katie opened the door and flipped on the light. Sliding hangers back and forth, she sorted through his collection and selected several shirts and sweaters. After arranging them on the bed, she studied Griffin, her head tilted to one side. She picked up a hunter green rugby shirt. "Now this just screams *Griffin*. Conservative, but in style."

"What about that one?" He pointed to a dark blue polo with the Oxford University crest on its pocket.

"You want to fit in, don't you?"

"Of course."

"Then never wear anything from a university twice as old as our country." She held out the rugby shirt. "Here—let me see this on you."

Griffin froze. Fumbling with the hem of his sweater for a moment, he shifted his feet, trying to work up his nerve. *Just take it off. It's no big deal.* He pulled his top over his head and tossed it on the bed. Trying to act nonchalant, he hitched his jeans higher and stepped toward her, reaching for the shirt.

Katie caught herself staring as he approached. She blushed and looked up.

"So, are you going to hand me that?" he asked, his face just as red.

"Sure."

Neither of them moved.

Then Griffin took another step and closed the distance. Katie tilted her head back. Their eyes locked. For a moment, they stood gazing at each other. Then, his hands at his sides, he bent over and kissed her. When she leaned closer, he wrapped his arms around her, breaking the kiss as he held her.

She laid her head on his shoulder, her breath tickling his throat as she sniffed his neck. "You smell like—" She took another whiff. "Like the ground on a warm day. After the snow melts."

"Is that good?"

"Very good."

They jumped apart at the sound of chairs scraping across the floor in the dining room below and the murmur of voices. Katie noticed the shirt still clutched in her hand; she hurriedly tossed it to Griffin. He snagged it in mid-air, yanked it over his head, and tugged it into place. They stared at the door, waiting.

"Katie!" Helen called from downstairs. "It's time to go!"

"Be right down, Mom," Katie called back. She reached over and adjusted his collar. "It looks good on you. Very—"

"Human?"

Katie laughed, and then snapped her fingers at the dog. Bear rose and padded over to nose Griffin's hand. Wagging his tail, he followed the girl out the door and down the stairs. Griffin trailed behind.

When they joined the others in the entryway, Basil raised an eyebrow. "Different shirt?" he said under his breath.

"Well, yeah. I mean, that's why we—"

Basil shook his head as he held the door open for his guests. "We'll talk about it later."

Griffin's Journal: Monday, January 10th

I hate it when Basil does that! He's so nosy. Asked me if I had changed my shirt in front of Katie. Like we were doing something wrong. Went on and on about appearances. And how our actions can lead people to make assumptions about us.

What. Ever.

It wasn't like I had taken my jeans off or anything. I told him he should watch TV once in a while. Seems like people are doing a lot more than just changing shirts these days.

Man, that got him going. The way he reacts to stuff, we might as well live in a monastery.

Oh. Wait. I think he did for awhile. During the fourteenth century.

How many more years until I can leave for college?????

Kissing Katie like that was awesome. Felt incredible. Powerful.

Katie's Journal: Monday, January 10th

I kissed Griffin tonight without a shirt on. I mean, <u>he</u> didn't have <u>his</u> shirt on. I could have stayed like that all night. Should I feel this way about him?

Do other teenagers know exactly what to do about all this and I'm the only one who's clueless?

Chapter Nine

"Basil, I'm leaving," Griffin yelled over his shoulder as he ran down the stairs, his book bag flopping against his hip. "Oops. My schedule." He whirled around and ran back up. Hurrying into his room, he snatched it off his desk and shot out again. He took the steps two at a time, skidded to a stop in the entryway, and snagged his jacket off the hook. "Basil?" he called again, his hand on the doorknob. He listened for a moment. *I guess he's on a mission. Except he always lets me know when he's taking off.* He shrugged, then stepped out the door and locked it behind him.

Pocketing his key, he headed down the steps and along the walkway, the snow crunching underfoot. The early sun glanced off the tips of roofs and trees; indigo shadows stretched across the street. *I'm glad I can catch a ride with Katie each day. Nice of Mr. Heflin to drop us off on his way to work.* As he reached the sidewalk, a breeze chilled the back of his neck. He stopped and turned around.

"That was cutting it a bit fine," Basil said, appearing on the porch with a faint pop. "I was afraid I might miss seeing you off on your first day."

"Where were you?" Griffin jogged back to join him.

"Why, I had an errand that couldn't wait. I thought you might want to take a few of these. Just in case." He pulled a small grocery sack out of his jacket pocket and handed it over.

Griffin frowned in confusion as he opened the bag and peered inside. "Oh, no way." He pulled out a box of granola bars. He grinned as he took a handful and shoved them into his book bag. "Remember when I used to hide these in my room? When I first came here?"

"Sadly, I do."

"You used to do sweeps once a week, sniffing around my room for rotting food. Remember the tuna sandwich I hid under the bathroom sink? Now, that was gross. Even for me." He laughed, shaking his head.

"You had a reason, lad. I certainly didn't blame you. Not after what Nicopolis did to you—withholding food as a punishment. But I'm grateful you can laugh about it now." He clapped a hand on Griffin's shoulder as he took the rest of the box back. "You've a rare gift, Fin. The ability to find the good in the bad."

"Like accepting my humanity?"

"Just like." Basil nodded and inspected the boy from head to toe. "Well, you look fairly presentable. Except for..." He reached out and swiped at Griffin's hair, trying to smooth it down.

"Don't!" Griffin ducked away. "Katie likes it this way." He glanced across the street and spotted Lewis Heflin idling his SUV, its engine rumbling unevenly with the cold. "They're waiting for me. I better go." He hefted his bag and started for the steps when Basil snagged his elbow.

"Be respectful to your instructors."

"I will." Griffin nodded goodbye, then dashed down the steps and across the street. Without looking back, he clambered in next to Katie.

Basil raised his hand as they drove away. Tilting his face toward the morning sun, he closed his eyes.

*　*　*

"Griffin Raine, Griffin Raine," the teacher muttered as he dragged a stubby finger down the list on his desk.

"Yes, sir. Raine with an e." Griffin waited near the teacher's desk, trying not to stare at the hairs growing out of Mr. Milton's ears. Glancing around the room, he squeezed to one side as the other students pushed passed him. A few eyed him with curiosity. Most ignored him.

Milton grunted. He began pawing through the chaos on his desk and came up with a pen, the tip brutally chewed. "You know, it's a real pain when kids decided to come to school *after* the semester begins." After locating Griffin's name, he ticked it off. With another grunt, he heaved his bulk out of his chair and rummaged in the cupboard behind him, finally pulling out a battered math book.

"Here." As Griffin started to take it, Milton held it up out of reach. "And I want it back at the end of the semester. In good condition. These things cost money, you know." He stared at Griffin, his eyes half hidden under a mane of graying hair.

Griffin stared back. "Right." He took the text and tucked it under one arm.

Milton looked down and studied the list again. "Says here you were home schooled."

"Yes, sir. My father—"

"Every student I've had that was home schooled was lazy. Or a troublemaker. Or both. So I'm going to keep my eye on you, Raine. With an e. Go take a seat."

Griffin nodded. He made his way toward the far corner of the class, ignoring the whispers and glances of the other students. He found an empty desk, then dug in his bag for some paper and a pencil. *Okay, knock it off,* he thought to himself, furious at the faint tremble in his hands.

He jumped when the bell rang. Two girls rushed in just as Milton reached the door. "Torrez and Barber. Since you two can't seem to have your butts in your seats when the bell rings, both of you have detention after school. You can practice punctuality." The girls exchanged frustrated looks, but said nothing. "Get here on time, people. It's not that difficult to use a watch." He picked up his attendance list.

As Milton barked out name after name, Griffin shifted in his seat. *Katie was right about him. Who'd the guy learn his people skills from? Darth Vader?* He sighed as he opened the algebra book and began thumbing through it. *And I'm going to be totally lost, even at the lowest level. I'm lucky we have study hall together. Because I'm going to need her help with—*

"Raine!"

Griffin jerked his head up.

Milton stood in the aisle, glaring at him. "You mind answering me when I take attendance? I called your name twice."

"Sorry—I didn't hear you." Out of the corner of his eye, Griffin caught a blur of movement as the entire class swiveled around to watch the assault.

"You got a hearing problem?"

"No, sir. I was just looking at the book and—"

"When I am talking, whether it's taking attendance or teaching a lesson, I suggest you stay focused. Got it?"

"Got it."

"You better have." Milton rapped his knuckles against his clipboard for emphasis. After an eternity, he snorted and turned away, stumping back down the aisle as he called out the next name.

Griffin kept his face expressionless. *Fire, I'm still not used to being called by that last name.* Slumping down in his desk, he ignored the smirks of the two boys in front of him.

By the end of class, Griffin's head throbbed with the effort to keep up with the lesson. When the bell rang, he scribbled the homework assignment on his palm, shoved his book and papers into his bag, and peeked at the map. He made his way out of the room and plunged into the crowd. Squeezing through the halls, he hurried across campus as fast as he could. He breathed a sigh of relief when he spotted Katie waiting outside study hall; he grimaced as he reached her side.

"That bad, huh?" she asked.

"I made a target out of myself the first five minutes." He leaned against the wall as he massaged his temple. "Milton hates me. Because I was *home schooled*. He made it sound like a disease or something."

"I told you it was a rough class."

"It's no *paradise*. And I'm *lost* already with today's homework." He raised his eyebrows and waited. "Get it?" At her blank expression, he elaborated, "*Milton? Paradise? Lost?*"

Katie groaned. "You are such a geek."

* * *

"What do you usually have?" Griffin studied the menu over Katie's head as they waited in line. The smell of fish sticks and bleach water drifted around them. He winced as the thunder of voices and clattering trays vibrated from the soles of his feet to the tips of his ears.

"Generally a sandwich. But there's a salad bar, too." Katie nodded toward the far end of the line. She leaned forward, one hand on his arm. "Since you're mortal now, are you okay to eat meat?" she whispered.

"Yeah, I'm good. No more reactions." As they inched forward, he scanned the room. *I wonder if...yup, there he is.* He spotted Nash Baylor with others of the football team at a corner table. The sandy-haired junior laughed as he shifted his bulk to one side to allow another player to join them. Still laughing, he glanced around. Spotting Griffin across the room, he straightened up for a better view. Their eyes locked. An undeclared warning flared between them before the junior shrugged and looked away. *I hope that means a stalemate*, Griffin thought. *Because now he'd really kick my butt in a fight.*

Finally reaching the front of the line, they filled their trays, Griffin gleefully ordering a hamburger and double fries. He snagged a small bottle of vinegar from the condiments table and followed Katie back to the common area. They chose an empty table along the wall. Griffin picked the chair facing the room.

"Hey, where's Carlee? I thought she had lunch with you?" he asked, sprinkling his fries. He glanced up at Katie's expression. "What?"

"Vinegar? On French fries?"

"It's a Brit thing. Basil got me hooked on the taste."

Katie tore her eyes away. "Her schedule changed at semester, so she has first lunch now." She opened her sandwich and removed the tomatoes with a shudder. "You want these?"

Griffin stabbed them with his fork and piled them on the patty before replacing the bun. "I never knew what I was missing, not being able to eat a burger." He took a bite, then chugged his soda. Swallowing the mouthful, he started to speak. "So when do you—"

Blinding pain ripped through his head. With a gasp, he dropped the burger and pressed a palm against his forehead, his eyes squeezed tight.

"Brain freeze?" Katie asked. "Well, that's what you get for gulping a cold drink like that."

He opened his watering eyes as the agony faded. Hitching in a breath, he blinked a few times. "Fire, that hurt." He picked up his lunch. Before he could take another bite, a voice spoke.

"Hey, guys." They looked up in surprise. Cas Navarre stood before them, balancing a tray piled with several slices of pizza. "Can I sit here? All the tables are full."

"Sure, let me move my stuff." Katie grabbed her backpack and shoved it under the table. "Griffin, this is—"

"—Cas Navarre. Yeah, we met yesterday. He gave me a tour." He smiled as the other boy put down his meal and joined them. "So you two know each other?"

"Cas is in science with me," Katie said. "He was my partner last semester on that big project."

Griffin's Fire

Cas picked up a slice of pizza and folded it in half. "You sure work fast, Raine. Only here half a day and you already got Heflin to eat with you," he said, shoving half the pizza into his mouth. He chewed a few times, then mumbled around the food. "She's got a boyfriend, you know. Some guy that doesn't go here."

Griffin reached under the table and clasped Katie's hand, squeezing her fingers. She peeked back at him, her eyes dancing. "Yeah, she told me all about him," he said to Cas. "Smart, athletic, and incredibly good-looking." He waited until Katie took a drink, and then added, "Like some kind of god was how she described him."

Katie spewed her water across her tray, hiccupping with laughter. She scrambled red-faced for a napkin.

"And that's what *you* get for gulping *your* drink." Griffin winced when she kicked his ankle in retaliation.

"Well, the rumor around school is that he took on four football players in a fight at Carlee Webb's party last month. And won. So I'd watch it if I were you." He took another bite, then froze, staring at them when they burst out laughing. "What?" he asked, his cheeks full.

"Griffin is my boyfriend. We live across the street from each other. That's how we met last summer." Katie reached over and lightly slapped Cas' arm. "Sorry about teasing you."

"*You* beat up Baylor and his gang?" Cas stuffed the last slice in his mouth and looked Griffin up and down. "No way."

Griffin shrugged. "Way."

The bell rang. They scrambled to their feet. After stacking their trays, they joined the throng squeezing through the double doors. When they reached the main hallway, they halted to one side.

"C'mon," Cas said, nodding toward an outside exit. "I'll show you a short cut around the outside of the building. It's easier to get to history that way."

"I better go." Katie smiled up at Griffin. "I'll meet you out front after school." She gave him a quick hug and dashed off in the opposite direction. The boys headed outside.

Darby Karchut

The winter-dry lawn crunched beneath their feet as they walked around the corner of the main building. Griffin looked at the other students also taking the same route. Jeans and hoodies and backpacks were almost a uniform. Some of the faces he studied mirrored his own feeling of *wrongness. I don't belong here. Not really. And maybe I'm not the only one.*

"Hey, you okay, Raine?"

"What? Oh, I'm good. Just thinking." Griffin forced a smile on his face as they headed inside.

* * *

"Where's the stupid art room?" Griffin broke into a jog as he raced down the deserted hallway. He flew around a corner, nearly bowling over Mr. Navarre.

"Whoa there." The counselor put out a hand. "Griffin, right?"

"Yeah. I mean, yes, sir." He shifted his feet and hitched up his book bag.

"Lost?"

Griffin nodded, and then dug his rumbled schedule out of his back pocket and handed it over. "I'm supposed to be in art." He wiped his forehead while Navarre studied the paper.

"You need to go back to the front entrance and take the stairs. Art is on the second floor."

"Okay. Thanks." Griffin blew out a breath and turned to go, then looked up in surprise when Navarre fell into step beside him.

"I'll go with you and let Zimmerman know why you're late."

Griffin smiled in relief as they walked along. After reaching the main hall, they trotted upstairs. The tang of turpentine filled the wide corridor. Several students, each equipped with easel and canvas, stood by a bank of windows, painting. Navarre stopped outside the first door and pulled it open, shooing Griffin in ahead of him.

"...and make sure you wrap it tightly so it doesn't dry out overnight," said a booming voice. A short, heavyset woman presided over the art studio from a raised platform like a high priestess, her tie-dyed apron crusty with dried clay. She flipped her long gray braids back as she stepped down and ambled toward them.

"James. Come to play in the mud?"

"Not this time, I'm sorry to say." He smiled, then gestured at Griffin. "Barbara, this is Griffin Raine. He's a new student, so still learning his way around. Griffin, meet Ms. Zimmerman."

Zimmerman nodded a welcome. "You picked a good time to join us. We just started a new unit yesterday. Ever work with clay before?" She waved goodbye as Navarre slipped out of the room, then guided Griffin over to a tall table off to one side.

"In a way."

"Well, store your pack under there and put on an apron. There's some over on the shelf."

She waited until he tied one around his waist, and then motioned for him to follow her into a large storage closet. A damp, earthy scent filled his nose. He smiled as he breathed it in. Blocks of reddish clay wrapped in plastic bags lined the shelves.

"What did you say your name was?"

"Griffin Raine."

"Well, Griffin, just yank off a wad and dive in. All we're doing today is playing with the stuff. Getting dirty using the tools nature gave us." Zimmerman held up her hands and wiggled her fingers. "All set? Okay, I'll leave you to experiment."

Spotting an open bag, he peeled off a chunk and carried it back to his table. The low hum of voices filled the room as students chatted with each other. Most worked in silence. The afternoon sun angling through the window warmed his back like an old friend.

For the first time in the day, Griffin felt himself relax. *I wonder what I should make?* He rolled the smooth, cool clay between his palms, patting it into a rough ball. After tossing it from hand to hand for a moment, he dropped it on the table with a plop. Standing on tiptoes, he pressed down and flattened it, then pulled the edges up on two sides. He squinted, studying it as he smoothed it with a thumb. Time slowed as he lost himself in the feel of the clay under his fingers, a rightness running through him.

He jumped when the teacher's voice called from across the room.

"Okay, let's clean up. By next week, you'll need to have a rough sculpture or bowl to practice some glazing and firing techniques." Zimmerman strolled around the room as she talked. "Then you'll discover the real magic of ceramics. When you mix the energy of heat with the strength of clay. Earth and fire—two very powerful elements."

Griffin blinked, the bliss within him fading as he stared down at his dirty hands.

Chapter Ten

Griffin's Journal: Wednesday, January 12th
I've got everybody fooled.

They all think I've accepted my fate. Katie's happy I'm in school with her. Basil seems less worried about me.

But yesterday in art class, when Zimmerman was talking about the Elements, it was like I woke up. And I realized I was just pretending. Being the good little Griffin everyone expects of me. Rolling over and taking the crap life keeps dumping on me.

Lapping it up with a smile on my face.

This is not how it's supposed to be! I can just feel it! I KNOW I'm supposed to be a Terrae Angelus.

But I'm not. And never will be.

Guess I should get ready to go—wouldn't want to be late for ~~hell~~ school.

* * *

Griffin frowned as he spun the dial on his locker a third time. He grimaced when the final clear the building bell clanged overhead. Reciting the combination under his breath, he jiggled the handle, then let out a growl of frustration when it refused to budge. One eye on the wall clock, he tried again. "Finally," he muttered at the satisfying click and swung the door open.

Darby Karchut

A hand reached past his ear and slammed it shut again.

Whirling around, Griffin came face to face with one of Nash Baylor's supersized teammates. He spotted Nash and another player a step behind. All three wore their brown and white letter jackets. A lingering student scurried past, her eyes averted, leaving the foursome alone in the hall.

"Remember me?" asked the older teen. He shoved Griffin against his locker.

"Why would I?"

"You lit my hair on fire."

"Sorry. You're going to have to be more specific than that."

"You think you're funny?" The teen shoved him again.

A high pitched whine began humming in Griffin's ears. "Get out of my face."

He started to push past when his assailant grabbed his shoulders and pinned him against the locker. The other two stepped closer.

"You're not going anywhere. Not until you show us what you got," he sneered. Without warning, he slapped Griffin, landing playful blows to both cheeks in quick succession.

Rage shot through Griffin like a jolt of electricity. A muscle in his jaw jumped.

"Well? Aren't you going to torch us?" A second round of slaps, harder this time. "Come on, freak."

Tasting blood from a cut inside his lip, Griffin shook his head. "I'm not stupid enough to start a fight in school. Are you?"

The teen raised his hand again. With a practiced move, Griffin blocked his assailant's arm and pushed him away.

"Aw, he's got nothing, Nash. Just like we figured."

Elbowing around his teammates, Nash crowded Griffin. For a long minute, they glared at each other, Griffin tipping his head back to keep eye contact.

At that moment, the rattle and clang of an approaching custodian's cart echoed from the far end of the hall. The sound of cheerful whistling accompanied it.

Griffin's Fire

"Come on, Nash. We better clear out. This loser's not worth it."

Nash nodded and turned to leave, then paused. He narrowed his eyes as if coming to a decision. "This is for making me miss the playoff game."

Then he drove his fist into Griffin's ribs before walking away.

Basil's Journal: Thursday, January 13th

Difficult mission this evening involving a bus traveling too fast and a sidewalk packed with people queuing up for a movie. I certainly could have used Griffin—never had a Tiro so wicked fast on his feet in an emergency.

However, he seems to be adjusting somewhat to school. He does appear rather tired and complained of a headache—even asked for aspirin. It's been difficult, these first few days, and his academic load is a bit of a challenge. Thank Heaven Katie is helping him with mathematics during their joint study hall.

But why would he need an icepack?

Griffin's Journal: Friday, January 14th

Am I glad it's Friday! It's only my first week and I already got a ton of homework. And sore ribs.

Cas wants to study for our history test next week. I might go over to his house this weekend.

I could use the break from Basil. He's smothering me! Keeps asking me how I like school. How I'm feeling. Am I making any new friends?

Give it a rest, dude!

There's something else going on with him, but I can't tell what it is.

I better clean up. We're going out for Mexican food to celebrate my first week.

Big. Whoopee. Deal.

Darby Karchut

Chapter Eleven

"Can I take the Saab tomorrow? Me and Cas want to study for our test next week."

Basil started to speak, then smiled politely as the waiter placed a basket of sopapillas and their bill on their table and left. He gazed at Griffin, an expectant look on his face.

Griffin frowned. "What?"

"What do you think?"

"Not a clue."

"Then try again."

Griffin gritted his teeth. "*May* I take the Saab tomorrow? *Cas and I* need to blah, blah, blah." He glared at the Mentor. "There. Happy?"

Basil stared back. "Drop the sarcasm."

Yeah, whatever, Griffin thought. He slouched back in his chair and began smashing his leftover black beans with his fork, the pulp oozing up between the tines like tar. He peeked out of the corner of his eye as a waitress sashayed past their table.

He's always on me about everything. He wasn't like this when I was his Tiro. All parental-like. We used to be a team. Equal partners on missions. He sighed and dropped his fork on his plate with a clink.

Feeling Basil's gaze, he looked up. "Okay, what'd I do now?" he asked, straightening in his chair as he wiped his upper lip. *That must be some hot salsa. I'm sweating like a pig.* His eyes widened at Basil's unexpected smile.

"Why, I'm simply admiring your performance. A fine example of a sixteen year old adolescent in a snit." He raised his iced tea glass in a salute. "Well done, indeed."

In spite of himself, Griffin snorted, then grinned. "Cheeky brat," he said, mimicking Basil's accent.

Chuckling, Basil leaned over and picked up the dinner check. He examined it for a moment, and then handed it to Griffin. "Here. Determine the tip for me. Twenty percent."

Taking the slip, Griffin jiggled his foot as he tried to remember the trick Katie showed him. "Should be five dollars and sixty cents. I think," he said after a moment and handed it back. Basil nodded, pleased, then placed some money on the table and led the way out.

They paused on the sidewalk. Above their heads, the restaurant's sign with its neon sombrero was lit up like a Christmas tree. Out of habit, they scanned the evening crowd.

A black-haired man, a little shorter than Basil and dressed in workman's clothes and mud-covered boots, brushed past them. A sheathed hunting knife hung from his hip. As the man looked at them in recognition, Griffin noticed his eyes, even in the dark, were an uncanny sky-blue.

"Basil," said the man, an Irish lilt to his voice. "A fair evening to ye."

"And to you, Gideon Lir," Basil responded with a nod. He watched as the stranger disappeared into the crowd.

Griffin craned his neck. "Who was that?"

"A hunter of a sort," Basil said, watching the man. "I wonder why his apprentice wasn't with him."

"Apprentice! You mean like..." Griffin pointed at himself.

"Terrae Angeli are not the only supernatural beings to inhabit High Springs, Fin. Gideon Lir is one of the Fey. Also known as the Tuatha De Danaan."

"You're kidding, right? I mean, the Tuatha De Danaan aren't real. They're mythical warriors, right? That hunt monsters or something?"

"This is a conversation for another time." Basil zipped up his jacket. "A bit nippy tonight. I believe we may get snow," he said, changing the subject. "Put your coat on, lad."

Griffin started to press, then he let the matter drop. "It's too hot. I should've worn my hoodie," he complained, bunching his jacket under one arm.

"Are you unwell?" Basil reached over to feel his forehead.

"Don't do that!" Griffin jerked his head away. "Anyway, I'm not sick. The food was spicy—that's all."

"You've been complaining about being too warm for several days—you might be running a low grade fever. Perhaps you should stay home tomorrow," Basil said as they crossed the street and headed through High Springs' central square. They strolled in silence along the dimly lit walk.

"Is that an order or a suggestion?" Griffin asked after a few minutes.

Basil started to reply, then paused. Enraged voices erupted from behind a copse of evergreens at the far end of the park. Muffled blows and cries of pain drifted toward them. "Stay put!" He raced away and vanished after a few steps. Nearby bushes flattened from the slap of wind.

Griffin waited. He frowned as he shifted from foot to foot, the vapors from his breath forming a halo around his head. The sounds of the brawl lasted another minute, and then stopped abruptly. He bounced up and down on his toes, peering into the dark.

He jumped when several voices bellowed in rage. Without thinking, he sprinted toward them. As he neared the grove, a shadowy figure staggered away cussing. Griffin ignored him and ducked between two thick spruces. He skidded to a stop, dodging to one side as another man stumbled past him, soaking wet.

Confused, Griffin stepped around the trees and shook his head. *I should have known.*

Basil stood in the center of the clearing. Both his hands were pointed at the remaining men sprawled on the ground. Water surged from his fingertips as he hosed them down. The needles on the nearby trees sparkled from errant water droplets turning to ice.

"Gentlemen," he shouted over their howls, "and I'm using the term quite charitably, brawling is a barbaric way to settle your differences." He increased the torrent when one of them tried to crawl away, driving the man back to the ground. Snow turned to slush around them.

After a few more minutes, Basil lowered his arms, then walked over and prodded the men with the toe of his shoe. "Now I suggest you hurry home and dry off before you develop hypothermia." He watched as they scrambled to their feet and squished away, hurling curses and suggestions of what he could do. "Yes, yes. I've heard *that* one before."

"I haven't," Griffin said from the shadows. "What's it mean?"

Basil spun around. "What are you doing here?"

"I came to see if you needed any help." He stepped around the puddle to Basil's side. "But I guess not. So what does—" He yelped when Basil reached out and flicked his ear twice. Hard.

"Ow! What was that for?" He glowered as he rubbed his head. "I didn't do anything."

"You disobeyed me." Basil shook out his hands, then dried them on his jeans. "I told you to wait. Then the next thing I see is you standing in the middle of the bloody fight. Not one of your more clever moves, Tiro." He started to walk away.

Sudden fury at Basil's use of his old title knocked Griffin back on his heels. "Hey! In case you've forgotten, I'm not your Tiro anymore." He flinched when Basil whirled around and grabbed him by the shoulders.

"Don't you understand? You may not be my apprentice in the Terrae Angeli tradition, but you are still—" He stopped, the muscle in his jaw jumping. Then, with a growl, he let go and stalked off into the night.

Griffin blinked in shock as he stared at Basil's retreating back. *What was that all about? He acted like...like...I don't know what.*

Darby Karchut

He swallowed. Breaking into a jog, he hurried to catch up. As he drew nearer, he slowed, keeping a step behind as the Mentor marched along. Silence hung between them like a thick fog all the way to the parking lot.

Reaching their car, Basil unlocked the Saab, then propped his elbows on the roof and stared into the distance. After a moment, he straightened up and tossed the keys across to Griffin.

"Here. Take the car. I'll be home later." He stepped back and vanished before Griffin could speak.

Basil's Journal: Friday, January 14th

I shouldn't have gotten so angry, but sometimes, I could wring his neck! What was he thinking? Showing up in the middle of a gang fight? I can't do my job if I have to worry about him, too.

And I know I overreacted when he said he's no longer my apprentice.

Griffin's Journal: Saturday, January 15th

Basil was royally pissed. Which is scary, because he doesn't get mad very often. But when he does – oy vey! He didn't come home until just before dawn. Guess I shouldn't have disobeyed him. Or told him I wasn't his Tiro anymore. Again.

Which was the same as telling him he wasn't my Mentor anymore.

I think that hurt his feelings.

* * *

Griffin hit save and swiveled around, then stood up. He stretched his arms over his head as he listened. *Basil must still be asleep. Good. I'll get the coffee started.* He snatched a tee shirt off the floor, sniffed it, and then shrugged. Tugging it over his head, he padded downstairs in his sweatpants, his bare feet soundless on the wooden treads. Out of habit, he skipped the squeaky fourth one.

As he started toward the kitchen, he stopped and spun around with a snap of his fingers. *Paper first. Because if I'm going to suck up to him this morning, I might as well do it right.*

Griffin slipped outside the front door, squinting up at the morning sun. He walked down the steps, across the snowy lawn to the sidewalk, and fished the paper out from under the sagging branches of the lone spruce.

After pulling off the plastic sleeve, he flipped to the sports page. "The Nuggets—what's the deal with them?" he muttered, shaking his head. He sauntered back, adding a second string of footprints in the snow like pearls on a necklace. After wiping his bare feet on the mat, he headed to the kitchen. He froze at the sight of the Mentor working at the sink.

Basil flipped on the coffee, then turned around and leaned against the counter, his arms folded over his chest. His eyes bored into Griffin. "Well, that was an unpleasant way to end the evening."

Griffin nodded and looked away. "S'my fault." He tossed the paper on the kitchen table. "Sorry I didn't do what you told me to."

"Apology accepted. And Griffin? Look at me." He waited until Griffin met his eyes, then continued. "You need to listen to me and obey me when we're in a dicey situation like last night. Understand?"

"Yes, sir."

"Please remember. I've flown quite a few solo missions. I *do* know how to take care of myself." He headed over the refrigerator. "What time are you going over to Cas Navarre's?" he asked as he pulled out juice and milk.

Griffin's jaw dropped. "I-I can still go? I thought I was, like, grounded or something." He hurried over to take both cartons from Basil and place them on the table. "He said around ten this morning. So I really can?"

"It appears I'm getting soft in my old age, but, yes, you can go." Basil stepped over to a cupboard and opened it. "Here." He tossed a box of Raisin Bran across the kitchen; Griffin snagged it in midair with one hand without looking as he poured cranberry juice into their glasses with his other. Basil stared thoughtfully.

"Say, does Centennial have a cricket team?" Basil sat down and poured cereal into both their bowls, then added milk. He glanced up. "Well? Does it?"

Griffin paused for a moment, speechless, then blinked. "Why, of course it does, Basil. It's right before the polo season. That way, the horses' hooves won't mess up the turf." He sat down and began eating; he spoke around a mouthful of food. "All joking aside, what's this about?"

"I just thought you might want to try a sport."

"If I do, it'll be track and field. Might go out for discus and shot put. Maybe javelin."

"Good choices. Any reason why track?"

Griffin took another bite and grinned as he chewed. "Three, actually. One—we practice on the same field as the girls' team. Two—Katie will be in the running events."

"And the third reason?"

"Katie will be in running *shorts*." He laughed at Basil's expression. *Cricket, my butt*, he thought to himself and finished his breakfast.

Chapter Twelve

Pulling up to the curb with a low rumble, Griffin checked the address over the house's red door. *Guess this is the right one.* He parked the Saab and grabbed his book bag, then headed up the neatly shoveled walk, the brick pavers steaming in the warmth of the winter sun. *It's a lot bigger than ours*, he thought as he approached the white two-storied house, *but I guess they need more room with four of them.*

Reaching the front step, he stopped and took a deep breath, then pressed the bell. The musical *ding-dong* echoed dimly through the door. After a few minutes, it swung open. The entryway was empty. Griffin frowned. A soft gasp came from somewhere around his knees. He looked down.

A little girl stood there, her cheek pressed against the edge of the door and her hands plastered flat on either side. She tilted her head back, wisps of black hair framing her face, and stared up at Griffin, wide-eyed. Her mouth formed a perfect O. Then, with a shriek of delight, she whirled around and darted away. "Mama," she called, disappearing around a corner. "Look, Mama! Angel!"

Griffin frowned as a stray thought whisked through his mind. Before he could catch hold of it, a woman appeared, her ebony hair pulled back in a smooth ponytail. The child scampered behind her on stockinged feet.

"Angel, Mama!"

Darby Karchut

"Hush, Tessie," she murmured as she approached, then smiled warmly. "Hello. You must be Griffin Raine. I'm Sylvia Navarre."

"Hi, Mrs. Navarre," he said, shaking her hand. He glanced down at the little girl bobbing on her toes beside her mother in a state of glee.

"And this is Theresa Marie. Our Tessie. But I guess you two already met."

"Yes, ma'am." He held out a hand to the child, then froze when she threw her arms around his knees.

"Angel!" she crowed, craning her head back as she gazed up at him.

"No, sweetie. This is Cas' friend, Griffin. Can you say *Griffin*?"

"Gwiffin!"

"Close enough," he said, cautiously patting her silky hair as her mother pried her loose, then scooped her up.

"Gwiffin angel!"

Mrs. Navarre sighed in exasperation. "I'm sorry. Ever since Christmas, she's had this *angel* obsession. We think it must have been our tree topper." She shifted the child to her other hip. "You might consider it a compliment, however," she said, her eyes twinkling. "You know—the old wives' tale about dogs and small children being able to recognize angels and all that?"

"I'm familiar with it."

She ushered him into the elegant hallway. "Son," she called after closing the door. "Griffin's here."

Footsteps sounded overhead. Cas appeared at the top of the stairs and leaned over the railing. "Hey, Raine!"

"Go on up, dear."

Griffin nodded politely and hurried up the stairs. Reaching the second floor, he followed his friend into his bedroom. He glanced around as Cas settled in front of his computer.

"I just need to finish printing out those notes for you."

"No worries," Griffin said. He spotted a history textbook and a binder in the middle of the rug. Dropping his bag, he pushed back the sleeves of his hoodie and sat down, sitting cross-legged as he got out his materials. As he flipped through his papers, he peeked around the room.

Shelves lined one wall, stuffed with books and stacks of magazines. A lacrosse stick leaned against the corner by the door and a guitar rested on a stand next to the bed.

A renaissance man. "What's that?" he said, pointing to a shield shaped plaque taking up most of the wall over Cas' desk.

"That? Oh, it's kind of like a family crest. Navarre is an old name from Spain."

"So is Cas your real name or is it short for something?"

The boy glanced over his shoulder. "Don't laugh, okay?" Griffin nodded. "It's short for Castile. A region in Spain." He turned back to his computer. "Weird name, huh?"

Griffin laughed. "Not any weirder than mine."

"You mean *Gwiffin?*"

"Hey!"

* * *

Wheeling the Saab around the corner to his street, Griffin nodded in time with the radio as he sang under his breath. He glanced over at Katie's house; he scowled at her empty driveway as he pulled into his own. *Bummer she's gone all weekend. I wonder how she did her first time skiing? Boy, I'd like to learn. Maybe Basil would let me take snowboarding lessons.*

He parked the car and hopped out. Whistling through his teeth, he hurried around to the front porch and bounded up the steps.

"Hey, I'm back," he called as he stepped inside. He stuck his head in the empty study, and then continued down the hall, hesitating at the foot of the stairs. "Basil?" He waited a moment, and then shrugged. After hooking his book bag over the newel post, he hurried to the kitchen and made a beeline for the refrigerator. A note stuck to the handle caught his attention; he nodded as he read it. "Okay. See you at dinner, then."

Rummaging through the fridge for a snack, he snagged a slice of ham and stuffed it in his mouth. He chewed as he search for a soda can. Coming up blank, he swallowed and reached for another slice.

White-hot pain tore off the top of his head.

He crashed to the floor. Eyes squeezed tight, he bent over and pressed his forehead against his knees with a moan. Each thump of his heart accentuated the torture. Needles stabbed at the inside of his skull. Digging his fingers into his temple, he begged silently for it to stop.

After an eternity, the agony began to lessen. His body went limp as the pain faded away. Griffin sucked in a shaky breath and opened his eyes, terrified it would return. When nothing more happened, he sat up and dragged his sleeve across his face.

Grabbing the handle on the refrigerator, he pulled himself to his feet and staggered to the sink. Bile burned in his throat. He spat down the drain, then rinsed his mouth under the faucet and spat again. *I hope that ham doesn't make an encore.* After a few minutes, he straightened up.

He grimaced when he broke out in a drenching sweat. Plucking his hoodie away from his body, he stumbled toward the back door. *Fresh air. I just need some fresh air.* He stepped out into the sunlight and made his way on wobbly legs across the yard.

Maybe Basil's right. Maybe I am *coming down with something. Or the meat was spoiled. Man, it felt just like...* He froze when the hairs on the back of his neck stiffened as Mrs. Navarre's words came back to him.

You know—the old wives' tale about dogs and small children.

Griffin shook his head, trying not to listen. Trying to deny the hope pressing against his heart. *Uh-uh. No way. Don't even go there.*

Unbidden, his arm lifted from his side.

Don't be stupid, said the Voice inside his head. *Put your hand down. You really think you're going to be* that *again?*

Griffin's Fire

He lowered his arm and closed his eyes. A breeze stirred his hair, cooling his brow.

But what if I am? And I don't know it? What if by some miracle—

Well, you're not. So stop being so desperate.

I could just try it, he argued back. *Fire, have a little faith.*

Faith? the Voice scoffed. *Faith in what?*

Faith that sometimes things turn out right, Griffin thought.

And when has anything ever turned out right for you? Have you forgotten Nicopolis? When has faith *gotten you anything decent in this world?* the Voice asked.

It got me Basil. A smile tugged at a corner of his mouth. *And Katie. And Miss Lena. And even—*

Oh, pul-lease. Stop before you hurt yourself. You're hopeless. And you're pathetic.

Griffin's eyes snapped opened in a flash of brown fire. "No. No, I'm not."

He looked down, hesitated for a moment, then dropped to both knees. Taking a deep breath, he raised his fist like a hammer and struck the earth in front of him.

The ground rippled outward like waves on a pond when a pebble is tossed. The ripples hit the nearby spruce tree. It shuddered, its needles showering down like spilled toothpicks.

Griffin stared in amazement at his hand. He slumped back on his heels, then raked his fingers across the surface of the ground next to him. The sod peeled up with a ripping sound and folded around itself like a jelly roll.

The aroma of fresh soil triggered the memory of his first moments of existence. A memory of the Earth sloughing away from his face and body as he emerged from the ground. The taste of the morning air as he took his first breath. A grove of pine trees had surrounded him, filtering the rising sun while a circle of Fire danced around him, as if in celebration. Griffin grinned, recalling the innocent joy of tossing fireballs into a nearby creek and laughing at the sizzling sound until the Guardians arrived an hour later, armed with clothes and smiles.

The oldest of the Guardians, his lined face wreathed by a gray-streaked beard, had approached him first. "Welcome to the world, young one." Cupping Griffin's chin gently in a wrinkled hand, the Guardian had gazed down at him, studying him.

"This one," he proclaimed after a few minutes, "shall be called... Larry."

"Are you quite certain *Larry* fits him?" one of the other Guardians asked, her brow puckered in confusion.

"Why, I think Larry is a fine name for him." The Guardian looked down. "What do you think?"

Griffin beamed and nodded.

The elder laughed, then shook his head. "I was just having a little fun," he said with a wink. He patted Griffin's cheek. "No, you shall be *Griffin*. 'Strong in faith.'"

Chuckling with relief, the other Terrae Angeli had helped him dress, then escorted him down the hillside to the Foundation's sprawling complex. There, in one of the guesthouses, he had spent a few happy days learning and practicing how to think and behave as a ten-year-old mortal.

Then Nicopolis arrived.

Griffin shook his head clear. *Don't think about him*, he ordered himself.

He scrambled to his feet and studied the pond tucked in the far corner of the yard. Narrowing his eyes, he focused on a large stone in the center of the wall as he cocked his arm back. The air shimmered around him.

With a *whoosh*, flames ignited in his hand. He curled his fingers around them, molding them into a glowing ball. Then he pitched it as hard as he could toward the wall. The fireball exploded on impact. Sparks flew into the air, then fell with a hiss into the water.

Griffin half-laughed, half-sobbed. A rising joy flooded his body, spreading to the very tips of his fingers and toes. "Well," he said hoarsely, "I guess I can check 'become an angel again' off my bucket list."

With a shout of exaltation, he leaped into the air and vanished.

Chapter Thirteen

Griffin's Journal: Saturday, January 15th

I don't know how. And I don't know why. But I'm an angel again.

I'm *me*, again.

And I'm not telling anyone.

Not Basil.

Not even Katie.

The risk is too high.

Basil would tear himself in half trying to keep it secret from Command when he knows he should report it. Like he didn't have a choice.

And even if we did keep it a secret, how could I go on missions with him? Be his apprentice? Be a real Terrae Angelus? Command would figure it out. And maybe send the Guardians after me again.

This may be a big mistake, but until I figure out what to do, I'll just keep playing mortal boy.

BTW, I seem to have out-grown my allergies! I didn't sneeze once while messing around with Fire!

Basil's Journal: Saturday, January 15th

I hunted with Sukalli today while Griffin was studying with his friend. Sukalli had heard a rumor that Nicopolis was spotted up in Denver. Unfortunately, by the time we arrived, he was gone.

Griffin's session with Cas Navarre must have gone well. He's more cheerful than I've seen in weeks. A pleasant change, to be sure.

Griffin's Journal: Sunday, January 16th

I'm still so jazzed I can't sleep. I almost broke down and told Basil yesterday afternoon, but stopped myself in time. I did whisper it to Bear this evening when I went over to feed him and take him out for a run, but I think he already knew.

Speaking of Basil—he's acting weird. Again. When I asked him about yesterday's mission, he said it was just a run-of-the-mill rescue and then changed the subject. He's a crappy liar.

Chapter Fourteen

"They're not in your bag?" Basil shouted from his study. He set his steaming mug to one side as he rifled through various folders scattered across the desk. "Which is where I told you to put them when you were finished," he said under his breath.

"No, I had them out last night because Cas wanted his notes back today," Griffin hollered back from the living room. He scrabbled through the newspapers on the coffee table, flinging one section after another aside in frustration; they drifted around him like giant snowflakes. With a growl, he dashed out of the room and up the stairs two at a time. "I'm going to check my room again."

Basil stepped into the hallway, stroking his chin as Griffin thundered about overhead. He eyed the book bag hanging from the newel post. Frowning, he reached into it and pulled out a book. He thumbed through it, then shook his head.

"Fin," he called up the stairs. "They were in your history text." He replaced the book. Taking a strategic position to one side of the hall, he held the bag out by its strap.

Griffin ran down the stairs. Grunting something, he snatched it out of Basil's hand, then raced past. He bolted out the front door and slammed it behind him.

"Why, thank you, Basil," the Mentor muttered to himself, heading back into his study. "How kind it was of you to assist me in locating my materials. Do have a jolly good day." He picked his cup off the desk and walked over to the window, finishing his coffee as he watched Lewis drive away, Katie and Griffin in the back seat. He started to turn away, then froze.

Two figures materialized out of the overcast morning. A gust shook the tree in the corner of the yard as they landed. They glanced around and headed up the walk toward the house.

Basil watched them through narrowed eyes. *Now what does she want?* He took a deep breath, set his cup down, and stepped around to the entry. "Mayla," he said as he opened the door.

"Hello, Basil," the Guardian replied. She waved a graceful hand toward the tall youth standing next to her. "This is Tiro Sergei, apprentice to Mentor Dimitri."

Sergei bowed his head once, his eyes the blue of a Siberian winter sky. "Mentor Basil. It's an honor to meet you."

Basil returned the nod with the slightest dip. He lifted an eyebrow at the duffel bag hanging from Sergei's shoulder. Suspicion began to buzz in his ears with a high, thin note.

Mayla broke the awkward moment. "May we come in?"

Opening the door wider, he stepped aside and gestured toward the living room. "Certainly."

"Thank you." She paused to brush snow off her overcoat, then swept past, her blue-black hair streaming behind her. She walked over to the chair by the fireplace and took a seat.

Dumping his bag on the floor beside him with a thump, Sergei perched on the edge of the sofa nearest her, then raked his fingers through his blond hair.

Basil shut the door and joined them, sinking down in the chair opposite Mayla. For a long minute, they sat in silence.

"And how is Griffin doing?" Mayla finally asked.

"Quite well. I'll be sure to give him your regards," Basil said, trying to mask the sarcasm and failing; he found he didn't care. Leaning back, he added, "He left a few minutes ago for school."

She shifted in her chair. "Yes, I know. I wanted us to talk while he was away."

Darby Karchut

Basil frowned and glanced over at Sergei. "What's this about, Mayla?"

She rose and walked over to the window, gazing out. "I'm afraid you're not going to like this, Basil." She turned around and lifted her chin. "Please know I tried to persuade Command to choose someone else. *Anyone* else. But the emergency team heading to the Middle East was short one Terrae Angelus and Dimitri's knowledge of the region is matchless. They left Denver early this morning."

Basil straightened, his hands clutching the arms of his chair while his coffee burned like acid in his stomach. He locked eyes with the Tiro. Sergei stared back unblinking, his handsome features expressionless. "Are you suggesting what I think you're suggesting?" he asked, wrenching his gaze back to Mayla.

"Not a suggestion, old friend. An order direct from Command."

"I already have a Tiro."

"No, you have a human teenager under your care. One who seems to be adjusting to life as a mortal."

"Mentor Basil..." Sergei began, but stopped when Mayla shook her head.

"Sergei will soon be completing his apprenticeship," she explained. "To suspend his training now until his Mentor returns would be detrimental to us all. Every Terrae Angelus is desperately needed in the field." She looked out the window again. "This world worsens daily, Basil, you know this. More and more of us are being injured or killed while on missions. We need every Tiro trained and promoted as soon as possible."

"Yet Command was quick enough to end Griffin's career." Basil rose in indignation.

Mayla's dark eyes narrowed as she whirled back. "We are trying to salvage that. Don't you think Sukalli and I regret what we had to do?" She threw up her hands in frustration. "Look, this is not about Griffin. It's about Sergei." Nodding toward the apprentice, she continued. "He's a Senior Tiro and the most gifted I've seen in years, so you'll need to do very little, if any, training. He just needs to hone his skills on missions."

Sergei stood up, his back ramrod straight as he faced them. "Mentor Basil, I'm willing to do whatever it takes to finish my apprenticeship. And I believe you'll find me a capable partner in the field," he added proudly.

"And Basil?" Mayla spoke again. "You should be aware that Command was making arrangements for Griffin to be sent to a human foster home." Before Basil exploded, she held up a hand and stopped him. "But I convinced them that you would be willing to take Sergei without resorting to…" Her voice trailed off.

"Without resorting to blackmail?" Basil shook his head in contempt, then stared into space as the mantel clock ticked away the minutes. Finally, with a sick feeling, he gestured for them to resume their seats. "Well, it appears I have no choice in the matter." He threw himself back down in his chair. *And I will not break my promise to Fin, that this will always be his home.* "Right," he said grimly. "Let's discuss details."

* * *

"See you, Dad," Katie said, sliding out of the back seat. She gave a wave as Lewis pulled away from the curb, then smiled up at Griffin as he hooked both their bags over his shoulder. "You know, I *can* carry that. I do it all day." They strolled through the school's courtyard, skirting the bronze mascot, its wings frozen in flight.

"I know, but your locker's right on my way. Plus I haven't seen you all weekend." He looked around and spotted a secluded corner under the covered walk by the library. "Come here." Reaching the spot, he dropped both bags on a patch of dry sidewalk and pulled Katie into his arms. "I haven't kissed you all weekend, either," he whispered in her ear, inhaling the scent of her vanilla shampoo.

"Then you better catch up," she whispered back and then lifted

Darby Karchut

her chin as she closed her eyes. After a moment, they stopped and pressed their foreheads together.

"Missed you," he murmured.

"Missed you more." Katie burrowed closer as he tightened his arms around her. After a moment, she raised her head and rubbed her nose against his warm cheek. "Sorry, but I'm freezing," she complained. "Can we go in now?"

"What a wimp," he said with a chuckle, letting go and picking up their bags. Hand in hand, they headed inside and snaked their way through the packed hallways toward her locker.

"So how was skiing?" he asked, maneuvering Katie in front of him as the crowd swelled, the drone of voices punctuated by the clang of locker doors. "Weren't you cold then?"

"Are you kidding?" Katie made a face over her shoulder and gave a mock shiver. "But once I got moving, it wasn't too bad. In fact, it was pretty great. I totally rock at snowplowing." She halted at her locker and twirled the dial while Griffin dropped her bag next to her feet. "I'll tell you more about it during lunch. How was your weekend?" she asked as she stuck her head inside and rummaged through the top shelf.

"Life changing." *Literally.*

"Sorry, I couldn't hear you. What did you say?" She pulled a notebook free and tucked it under one arm as she glanced up at the hall clock. "Oh, no, the bell's about to ring. I better go." She slammed the door shut, gave Griffin a quick hug, and started down the hall.

"Katie! Your pack!" Griffin snatched it off the ground as she turned back. With a quick heave, he tossed it to her, just missing the head of another student.

With an *oof*, she caught it in both arms like a football and grinned. "See you next period," she called and dashed off.

"Later," he yelled back and smiled after her. Noticing the halls emptying around him, he spun around and ran to his math class.

He shot through the door. His bottom hit his desk seat just as the bell rang.

Letting out a sigh of relief, he began digging through his bag, his mind racing. *I wonder if I should at least tell Katie. She'd be happy about it. And I know she would keep it a secret for me. But what if she slipped and accidentally told someone. Like her mom or dad. And they might tell Basil. Then he would have to—*

"Oh, no—my homework." He flipped frantically through his math book, finally turning it upside down and flapping the pages. When that yielded nothing, he yanked out his folder and began checking every page, a sinking feeling in his stomach. *Crap*, he thought. *Crap, crap, crap.* He scrambled faster at the sound of Milton lowering the white screen, the rollers squealing with age.

"Shut your yakking, people. Right now," Milton said. "Austin, hit the lights." He hoisted himself up on a tall chair at the front of the class and flipped on the overhead projector next to him. "You know the drill. Exchange worksheets with someone next to you. And make sure you use a red pen or pencil to correct this time. This isn't middle school." He slapped the first transparency down as the rustle of papers filled the room.

"Mr. Milton?" Griffin glanced over in dismay as the girl next to him waved her hand. "I don't have anyone to trade with."

"Switch with Raine."

"He didn't do his."

Griffin glared at her, then looked up. "I *did* do it. I think I left it at home."

Milton sneered as he leaned back and linked his hands across his ample belly. "Well, well, Raine-with-an-e. Only been here a week and you're already slacking off." With a cold gleam in his eye, he lowered himself out of the chair and made his way down the aisle. Reaching Griffin, he bent over and rested his meaty hand on the desk. "Just like I predicted," he said, his breath coffee-sour as he exhaled in Griffin's face. "You think the rest of the world should wait until you're in the mood to do your work." He thumped the desk, sending Griffin's math book sliding over the edge. "That homework better be turned in before school in the morning. And don't expect credit for it."

Griffin locked eyes with Milton, refusing to back down. He clenched his fist under the desk.

Milton stared at him for a moment more, the tension humming between them. Then he pushed away and stomped to the front of the room. "The rest of you get busy."

Griffin watched him walk away. He tightened his lips as he waited for his stomach to unknot. Then he reached down and picked his book off the floor.

Chapter Fifteen

Griffin leaned over the sink as he scrubbed away at the residual clay under his nails. *I'm glad I got art last period*, he thought, watching the murky water swirl down the drain. *And not right before lunch.* He looked at the restroom stall reflected in the mirror. "So how tough is our history test going to be?"

A toilet flushed. Cas swung open the door and joined Griffin at the next sink. "Tough enough. They always are. Make sure you review the notes about what was going on in England at the time. The Enlightenment, John Locke, and all that."

Griffin nodded absently. *John Locke—I think Basil knew him. I'll have to ask.*

Cas finished washing his hands and pulled a towel from the dispenser. "Want to come over and study some more?"

"Uh, no thanks. Going to hang out with Katie this evening. If I can." Drying his own hands, Griffin added. "She was gone all weekend skiing."

"Man, she's got you so trained." He laughed, then ducked as Griffin threw a sopping ball of paper towels at him. "Ah, the truth hurts." With a grin, Cas headed out the door. "See you tomorrow."

Griffin nodded goodbye. He left a moment later and hurried across campus; he brightened when he spotted Katie rummaging through her locker. "You ready?"

"Listen, would you mind if I didn't walk home with you today? Carlee had a fight with Zach and she needs to talk so we're going over to Oh-Be-Joyful for a double mocha." Katie pulled her jacket free. "Plus, I haven't spent much time with her since the semester started."

"Can't she go emote to someone else?" He slumped against the next locker.

"I'm sorry, but Carlee really needs me." She smiled as she reached over and squeezed his arm. "You look like an abandoned puppy."

"Yeah, well, I feel like one."

"I better go. Carlee's waiting for me at the front of the school. But come over tonight if you can." She started away, but Griffin snagged her elbow and pulled her back.

"I think you forgot something." He glanced around, and then gave her a quick kiss. "There. That should last me until this evening." Katie laughed and hurried away. Griffin watched until she disappeared around the corner, then headed in the opposite direction and out through a side door.

Walking home under a cloudless blue sky, the sun already low in the horizon, he made his way through the neighborhood and across the park. When he reached the suspended tire, he gave it a push. Leaning against one of the support posts, his thoughts spun around in his head like the swing.

I wish I knew how all this happened. And why it happened. Like did my angelic powers return or did my mortality fade away? Or was it a combination of the two? Basil would know. Or would know how to find out. This is the hardest part. The time I need him the most is the time I'm afraid to go to him. I wonder what Command would do if they knew. Would they turn me again? Fire, it hurt so bad before. I don't think I could stand going through that again.

So what does this make me? Angel? Human? Half and half? Is this where the legend of fallen angels come from?

He shook his head and left the park. Reaching his front yard, he checked the mailbox, and then hurried along the walk. Jogging up the steps, he paused when the front door opened.

An older boy stepped out. He pushed the screen door open with his toe as he juggled a large box in his arms. His blue eyes narrowed in recognition. "Oh. You must be that mortal—"

"W-who are you?"

"I'm Sergei. Mentor Basil's new Tiro."

Chapter Sixteen

An invisible fist punched Griffin in the chest. His mouth opened and closed soundlessly as a voice screamed inside his head. *Tiro? Basil got another Tiro?* "Where is he?" He gripped the porch rail for support.

"Upstairs. He's trying to—" Sergei stopped when a tall figure appeared behind him in the entryway. They both watched as Basil eased out the door.

"Sergei, go ahead and take that box to the garage, would you?"

"Of course." Sergei hoisted the box higher and brushed past Griffin. He trotted down the steps and disappeared around the side of the house.

Basil opened the screen wider. "Come inside and I'll explain everything."

Griffin hesitated, then stalked past him and into the study. He took a stance in the center of the room, his back to Basil as he stared into the cold fireplace. "Why?" he asked over his shoulder, his lips stiff.

"Because Sergei's Mentor was already halfway around the world on an emergency assignment." Basil closed the door and walked over to his desk, balancing a hip on the corner of it. "And there was simply no one else to take him."

"For how long?"

"A year or two. Perhaps less, depending on how soon he's promoted."

"So what happens to me?"

"Not a thing, lad."

"Yeah, right."

"Fin, look at me."

Griffin shook his head, unwilling to face his Mentor. He clenched his jaw when Basil rose and laid a hand on his shoulder, giving him an affectionate shake.

"Now, before you fall apart any further, do you recall the conversation we had last autumn? The night you and Katie attended that carnival at school?"

Griffin nodded once.

"Do you remember what I promised you?"

"Yeah."

"Remind me. Please."

"That…um…that no matter what happens, this is my home. For as long as I want."

"Right. And have I ever broken a promise to you?"

"No, but—" Griffin stopped at the soft knock.

"Mentor Basil?" Sergei called, his voice muffled by the closed door. "Shall I take those other boxes out to the garage?"

"Would you, please?" They listened as his footsteps faded away.

"What's he doing?" Griffin asked. A sudden weariness dragged at him. He dropped his book bag on the floor and sank down on the sofa.

"Tidying the guest room. You two will need to share the adjoining bathroom."

"Wow, lucky me. So, does he know about what happened?" He made a face when Basil nodded. "I thought so. He called me 'that mortal' when we first met."

"Really? Odd." Basil frowned for a moment, and then straightened. "Well, it is time you two were introduced properly. And then we'll discuss house rules."

Griffin let his head fall back against the cushions. "It's going to be so weird having another Tiro around."

"Just think of him as an older brother."

"More like a step-brother."

Basil winced. "Not the way I would describe it." He tilted his head toward the door. "Come along."

Griffin rolled his eyes as he heaved himself up. "He better stay out of my room," he declared as he opened the door.

Basil's Journal: Monday, January 17th

Due to an abrupt re-assignment of his Mentor, Tiro Sergei will be completing the rest of his apprenticeship with me. Reports indicate that he is one of the best and the brightest of his generation. He had passed his *Proelium* in four minutes. Fastest time on record.

We spent most of the afternoon and evening getting to know one another and establishing a few rules. And modified our cover story. Sergei will be my nephew staying with us while his father is deployed overseas. A familial connection makes sense, since he's a Wind and Water and the physical similarities are obvious. I also explained the nature of our friendship with the Heflins, including Griffin and Katie's relationship. Sergei seemed surprised I would allow it.

We're on call beginning tomorrow morning. I'm curious to see what he can do.

Naturally, Griffin was stunned about all this. Both lads were quite reserved around each other during dinner, but that's to be expected. I hope they can be friends, even though Sergei is an earth year older than Fin.

Katie's Journal: Monday, January 17th

Griffin just left. He told me about Sergei. He acted like it was no big deal, but I could tell it shook him up. He only stayed a few minutes because he had to get back to study for his history test, but he did say I should let Mom and Dad know.

When we said good night, he held on to me for a long time.

Griffin's Journal: Monday, January 17ᵗʰ
He got a new Tiro.

* * *

Basil stuck his head around Griffin's half opened door. "Require any assistance, young scholar?" He stepped into the room.

Griffin closed his history book with a clap and rolled off his bed. "Nope, I think I'm ready." He stepped over to his desk and tossed the text on a stack of folders, then fell backwards on the bed, his bare feet dangling off the end. "What a rotten day," he said to the ceiling.

"Bloody awful, eh?"

"Are you kidding?" He counted on his fingers. "I forgot my math homework. Then Milton got in my face about it in front of the whole class. I have a major test in history tomorrow. And Katie went for coffee with Carlee instead walking home with me."

"I noticed you didn't mention the gorilla."

"The *what?*"

"The eight hundred pound gorilla standing in the middle of the room. The one you're pretending not to notice."

"You mean Sergei, don't you?"

"Do you want to talk about it?"

Griffin shrugged.

Basil walked over and grabbed the swivel chair. Spinning it around, he sat down and leaned back, one elbow resting on the desk. "Well, I wish I could ease things for you."

Griffin blinked at the sad tone in the Mentor's voice and sat up. "I know. It's just life, I guess. You can't always make it better for me."

"But that's what I do. I *am* a guardian angel, after all," Basil joked.

Griffin grinned back. "A guardian angel? Even for me?"

Darby Karchut

"Oh, no, that would take a full time specialist. At the very highest level." He smiled as he stood up and headed out the door. "Sleep well," he added, closing it behind him.

As Basil turned around, he noticed Sergei coming up the stairs. "Sergei. You're up late."

"I was getting some water." He held up a plastic bottle.

"Right. By the way, we are on call beginning tomorrow at seven."

"Seven, then. I'll be ready." He gestured toward Griffin's room. "And I'll be careful not wake him in the morning."

"Oh, I don't believe that will be a problem. He's usually the first one up since he leaves for school quite early."

"Then I'll make sure to stay out of his way. I wouldn't want to make the boy late." He nodded politely. "Well, good night, Basil," he said and headed to his room.

Basil stared after him for a few moments, then walked downstairs, a slight frown on his face.

Chapter Seventeen

Drying his hair in front of the mirror, Griffin eyed the pale line bisecting his right eyebrow. *My battle scar. At least that's what Basil calls it. "All warriors have a collection of old wounds, Fin".* His eyes shifted to a faint mark on his lower lip. *Guess that's a battle scar, too.*

He wiped his neck and chest, flung the towel over the shower rod, then hurried into his room. After pulling on jeans and a long-sleeved tee shirt, he perched on the rumpled bed to tie his shoes. Hopping up to smooth the quilt, he heard Sergei's door slide open on the other side of their connecting bathroom, then shuffling footsteps. Out of the corner of his eye, he spied a figure standing in the doorway.

"Finished?" Sergei yawned, scratching his stomach through his tee, his pale hair sticking up on one side of his head.

"Yeah, go ahead."

Sergei grunted and left, rolling the door closed behind him. Almost immediately, it opened again. He stuck his head out. "Your wet towel is still in here."

"Oh. Sorry."

As Griffin started for the bathroom, Sergei yanked it off the rod. Balling it up, he tossed it through the door.

"Hey!" Griffin caught it just before it smacked him in the face. "It has to dry."

"Well, I can't take a shower with it hanging there. It's in my way."

Griffin shook out the towel with a snap, then stalked past Sergei. He hung it on the hook next to the door. "Happy now?"

"Thrilled beyond belief." Sergei made a shooing motion with his hand. "Now if you'll excuse me—some of us are on call." He waited until Griffin backed out and banged the door closed in his face.

"Jerk," Griffin muttered. He stomped out of his room and down the stairs to the kitchen. Still fuming, he opened the cupboard open and grabbed a packet of oatmeal. Snagging a clean bowl from the dishwasher, he poured the oats and added water. He headed for the microwave, then stopped and peeked around. All clear. Wrapping his hands around the dish, he tensed his body in concentration.

Steam began rising as the cereal cooked; the aroma of warm cinnamon spiced the air. While he waited, he scowled as he gazed out the window at the gray dawn. "It was *my* bathroom first, you…"

"Is this a private conversation?" Basil appeared in the doorway, fully dressed and his hair spiky from his shower.

Griffin jumped. The bowl slipped from his fingers. He winced as it shattered in the sink. Half-cooked oatmeal splattered everywhere. "What? No. Just, um, making some breakfast." He turned around, trying to block the sink with his body. "You're up early." *I hope he didn't see anything.*

Basil walked over to Griffin and crowded him as he leaned around. "Seven o'clock shift." He peered down at the mess, then shrugged and stepped away. He checked the coffee machine before turning it on. "Well? Are you going to clean that mess?"

"Oh, yeah. Right." Griffin let out a silent sigh of relief and gathered up the broken bits of crockery. He tossed them in the trash and rinsed the oats down the drain.

Griffin's Fire

Basil leaned against the counter as he waited for the coffee to brew. "Since I'm up, what would you say to scrambled eggs and toast?"

"Just toast, please." Griffin grabbed a glass and headed to the refrigerator, helping himself to some juice. Pulling out the butter and jam, he placed them on the table and then checked the kitchen clock. "It's seven right now."

"I'm aware," Basil said. He dropped two slices into the toaster and poured himself a mug of coffee.

"So shouldn't he be here?" Griffin asked. "Ready to go?" He sat down at the table, glass in one hand.

"It's not really your concern, lad."

Griffin blushed. He gulped half of his juice to hide his embarrassment, then jumped up. "I better get my stuff." He walked out of the kitchen and up the stairs. As he reached the upper level, Sergei stepped out of his room, dressed in jeans and a thick, white sweater. For a moment, they eyed each other, Sergei a few inches taller than Griffin.

"Don't you need to be leaving for school?"

"Don't you need to be ready for your shift?"

Sergei's blue eyes darkened. "I don't need a *Lucy* telling me my job." He pulled his door shut behind him with a bang.

"A w-what?"

"A Lucy. Short for Lucifer," Sergei said with a sneer. "You know. A *fallen* angel."

"Where did you—"

"Don't you know? That's what the other Tiros are calling you."

"No, they're not! You're only saying that to—"

Sergei laughed at Griffin's thunderous expression. "Oh, get over yourself. It's just a joke." He shoved past and headed downstairs.

Bitterness filled Griffin's mouth. He stormed into his room and gathered up books and notes from his desk. He stuffed them in his book bag as he seethed at Sergei's words. *Forget them—I know what I am. And I don't care if nobody else knows*, he lied to himself. He hurried down the stairs and along the hallway, and then paused in the archway. "I'm leaving," he shouted toward the kitchen.

"No, you're not," Basil called back. "Breakfast first."

"I'm not hungry." Griffin took his goosedown vest from the hook and reached for the doorknob, hoping for a quick getaway.

"I don't believe I care. And I refuse to bellow across the house at you any longer. So in here. Now."

Griffin groaned. He tossed his stuff on the bench and stalked toward the kitchen. Taking a stance in the doorway, he tried again. "I don't want to make Mr. Heflin late."

"You have twenty minutes. And I know from past experience you can wolf down an entire meal in eleven, so I believe we're quite safe." Basil pointed with a spatula toward a full plate on the table across from Sergei. "Eat." He turned back to the stove, the sound of sizzling eggs filling the kitchen.

Griffin threw himself in the chair, ignoring Sergei's smirk. Tearing the toast in two, he gobbled a half, washing it down with the rest of his juice. "Now can I go?"

Basil waved a hand in dismissal. Griffin raced out of the kitchen. The front door slammed closed a moment later. The Mentor shook his head as he scraped eggs onto a plate and handed it to Sergei.

They ate for a few minutes, then grimaced in unison when the beam of Light shot across the kitchen, the voice within almost inaudible. Basil chewed as he listened. "Right," he said as it faded. He rose from the table, gulping a final swig of coffee. "Sergei, our jackets. We'll leave through the back."

Katie's Journal: Tuesday, January 18th

That new Tiro must be a real creep. Griffin was so pissed when he got in the car this morning—even my dad noticed something was wrong. Dad had us meet him at his office on campus after school so we could catch a ride home. Pretty handy that my school and his work are just a few blocks apart. While we waited for Dad to finish teaching his last class, we went over to the College's café for a snack, and then back to his office and got our homework done. I think Dad did that so Griffin wouldn't have to go home right after school.

Griffin's Journal: Tuesday, January 18th

Sergei's a jerk.

Ser-jerk.

The only good thing today was that Mr. Heflin let us hang out at his office at the College after school. I wish I could live with the Heflins instead of Basil.

Basil's Journal: Tuesday, January 18th

Sergei is good. Very good. I had him fly solo so I could observe. He landed on the roof, hosed down the chimney fire, then escorted the family to safety all in under twenty minutes. The home had only minor smoke damage. He even rounded up the Pug to the delight of the elderly couple. And to the delight of the Pug. Sergei was quite irritated when little Joey accidentally urinated on his trousers.

Griffin would have laughed.

Sergei did not find it amusing. At all.

I did.

The fire trucks had very little to do, except check the house for safety and contact the couple's son.

Sergei and Griffin seem to be getting along reasonably well. I believe this may be a fairly smooth transition.

Basil's Journal: Friday, January 21st

Well, I was dead wrong.

There's been a great deal of tension between those two all week. Thank Heaven it's Friday. We need a weekend to relax and regroup.

Darby Karchut

I believe we'd all enjoy a dinner out tonight. Perhaps at our favorite Mexican restaurant.

* * *

"For Heaven's sake." Basil halted in the hallway and patted his pockets. "I left the keys in my room. You two go ahead and get in the car." He jogged back up the stairs two at a time while Sergei and Griffin headed out the front door.

They marched in silence down the steps and around the corner of the house to the Saab parked in the driveway. Gravel and ice crunched under their feet. Reaching the car, they halted by the passenger door and eyed each other for a moment. Simultaneously, they both lunged for the handle.

"Shotgun," Griffin called, grabbing it first. He started to open the door, but Sergei slapped a hand on the doorframe and slammed it closed.

"I don't think so. *Children* in the back." He elbowed past and blocked it with his body.

"Yeah, whatever." Griffin pushed at Sergei. "Get out of the way."

Digging in his feet, Sergei gave a shove, sending Griffin sprawling. "What a klutz." He laughed as he fumbled behind him for the handle.

Griffin scrambled to his feet. "You jerk." He launched himself, punching wildly.

"Oooh—somebody's got a temper. Do you always throw a fit when you don't get your way?" Sergei swatted Griffin's fists aside with ease.

"Shut up!" Griffin swung again, cursing under his breath as his feet skidded on a patch of ice.

"I can see why you failed your *Proelium*. You suck at fighting."

"And you just plain suck." Griffin lowered his head and barreled into Sergei. He landed a couple of jabs.

Then the Tiro nailed him in the chest with a pile driver of a blow.

Breathless, Griffin doubled over. Pain lanced through him as he tried to pull air into his lungs. "I'm going kill you," he wheezed, wrenching himself upright.

"Bring it on, *Lucy*."

Blood thundering in his head, Griffin charged once again, blind to everything but the desire to hammer his fists into Sergei's sneering face. Suddenly, his feet left the ground as a large hand grabbed the collar of his vest and yanked him away.

"GRIFFIN!" Keeping a firm hold, Basil glared at them. "By the Light! What is going on here?"

Before Griffin could say anything, Sergei raised both hands, patting the air. "Basil, it's my fault entirely. Some good natured teasing got out of control. Don't blame him." He chuckled and ruffled Griffin's hair before he could duck away. "You know how boys are at this age. They overreact to everything."

"Why, you piece of—" Griffin lunged again, but Basil caught him around his chest, lifting him back off his feet. He flailed his arms and legs in an attempt to break free. "Let me go!"

Basil gave him a rough shake. "That is enough." He swung Griffin around and propelled him toward the house. "Go inside and cool off." He gave him another push when Griffin refused to budge. "Now."

With a final glower at Sergei, Griffin stormed off, Basil on his heels after ordering Sergei to wait in the car. Finding the front door locked, Griffin gave it a savage thump with his fist, rattling the iron knocker.

Without a word, Basil reached around him and unlocked the door. As soon as it was open, Griffin bolted inside and whirled around, his arms flung wide and his face dark with fury. "He started it. He keeps calling me a Lucy and—"

"Someone teasing you is no excuse for the physical assault I just witnessed."

Darby Karchut

"But he's the one who—"

"For Heaven's sake, Griffin," Basil said, holding up his hand to forestall any further argument. "Sergei's been here less than a week and this is how you behave? I understand there have been some problems, but I never thought it would come to a brawl in the bloody driveway."

"But he—"

"So consider yourself grounded. We'll talk when—"

"Grounded? For how long?"

Basil ignored the rude tone. "I'll inform you when I've decided. Now Sergei and I are going to dinner. We'll bring you something back. Until we return, you're to stay in your room."

For a long minute, they glared at each other, both refusing to surrender.

Griffin raised his chin.

Basil raised an eyebrow.

"You've a choice," the Mentor said in a cold voice. "Go. Or be hauled." He took a step forward.

Feeling tears of frustration prickling his eyelids, Griffin turned and bolted up the stairs. Reaching his darkened room, he kicked a stray shoe at the bathroom door with a thud, then flung himself on the bed.

Outside, the Saab rumbled to life. He rolled off the mattress and walked over to the window; he watched in a black rage as it backed out of the driveway, then drove away. As the red eyes of the taillights disappeared around the corner, he leaned his forehead against the cold pane.

"I hate him," he whispered through gritted teeth, his breath fogging a patch on the glass. He glanced over at Katie's and sighed at her unlit house. He forced the window open with a bang, and then clambered out. Perched on the steep roof, Griffin wrapped his arm around his knees and stared down at the empty street. "I hate him."

Griffin's Fire

Chapter Eighteen

Basil's Journal: Friday, January 21st
Griffin took a swing (actually it was several swings) at Sergei this evening, so I grounded him. I know he was angry, but I have zero tolerance for that kind of behavior. Sergei rubs him the wrong way, but that is no excuse.

I also ordered Sergei to stop calling Griffin 'Lucy.' It's demeaning and I know exactly why he's doing it. I have zero tolerance for *that* kind of behavior, too. My new Tiro is certainly a gifted Terrae Angelus, but he is overly-proud of his abilities and has a condescending attitude toward Griffin.

* * *

Basil yawned as he shrugged into his robe and ambled toward the stairs. *It appears I'm not the only one who slept in this morning*, he thought, glancing at the closed doors while he knotted his belt. *Although Griffin is probably awake. Just sulking in his room. Maybe I should check on him and inform him he's only grounded until tomorrow.* He tapped lightly, then eased the door open.

"What in Heaven's name?" Hurrying around the bed and across the room to the window, Basil shoved the drapes aside and closed the sash, his breath alarmingly visible in the chilly room. He perched on the edge of the bed next to the figure buried under the quilt. "Fin?" He waited as Griffin stirred and pushed the covers off his face.

"What's wrong?" he slurred, looking around bleary-eyed, his hair like a hedgehog's.

"That's what I would like to know." Basil frowned as he studied him. "Were you aware that you had fallen asleep with your window wide open? Aren't you freezing?"

Griffin pulled his arms out from under the covers and knuckled his eyes. "Nah, I'm good. Anyway, it's your fault," he complained, his voice hoarse with sleep.

Basil raised his brows. "Mine? Why is it my fault?" He settled back on the bed, his hands tucked inside his sleeves for warmth.

"The bean burritos from last night."

"So?"

"So I had gas. I had to open the window or I would have suffocated from the smell."

"Charming." Basil grimaced and stood up. He paused, watching as Griffin yawned and stretched. "Since you're awake, come downstairs. I want to talk with you about yesterday evening."

"The fight?"

"Yes, the fight. But coffee first." Basil headed out the door.

Griffin kicked off the covers and stretched again, cracking his back with a satisfying pop before rolling out of the bed. After pulling on sweatpants and a tee shirt, he made a detour to the bathroom, then dragged himself downstairs and into the kitchen. The coffee machine finished its grumbling while Basil fetched two mugs from the cupboard and spoke over his shoulder. "Have a seat."

He poured the coffee, adding milk to one, and handed it to Griffin before joining him. After a few sips, he placed his mug on the table and leaned forward on his elbows, pining Griffin with his eyes.

"I am *extremely* disappointed in your behavior last night," Basil said. "I will not tolerate brawling. If you two cannot resolve problems on your own, then talk with me. Understand?"

"Yes, sir."

"And you should know I have also spoken with Sergei about his attitude toward you. I demand you both treat each other with respect."

"I will if he will."

"Griffin!"

"All right. All right. I'll make nice." Griffin sipped his coffee. "So how long?"

"How long what?"

"How long am I grounded?"

"Until..." Basil paused, then relented. "Until about ten minutes ago." He shook his head ruefully as Griffin's face lit up.

"Really? Thanks, Basil!" *I can't wait to call Katie*, he thought gleefully as Basil continued to speak. *Going to spend the whole weekend together and—* "Wait, what did you say?"

"I said why don't we have the Heflins over for dinner tonight? Let them meet Sergei and vice versa."

Griffin made a face. He twisted it into a fake smile when Basil cocked an eyebrow at him. "Capital idea, old boy. Jolly good."

Basil reared back at Griffin's imitation with a look of umbrage. "I do *not* speak that way. And you are stereotyping."

"That's *exactly* how you talk." Griffin pushed away from the table and headed over to the coffee maker, fetching the carafe. "So are you guys on call today?" he asked as he emptied the pot into their cups and sat back down.

"Thanks, Fin." Basil swirled his coffee around, an old habit. "No, we're off until Monday."

A figure appeared in the doorway. "Tell me there's some coffee left," Sergei said as he staggered into the kitchen. He shuffled over to the table and fell into a chair, his eyes half shut.

"Good morning, Tiro."

Sergei blinked as he looked around. "What?"

"I said good morning. It's customary to greet others when you walk into a room." Basil waited.

Griffin cradled his mug, enjoying the scene, until he felt Basil's stern glance. He looked down and took another drink, trying not to smile.

"Oh. Right. Morning." Sergei yawned, then peered at their mugs. "So is there any left?"

"I don't believe there is. You're welcome to make more. Coffee's in the tin on the counter."

Sergei let loose an exaggerated sigh, and then heaved himself up and stomped over to the sink. He muttered under his breath as he fumbled the lid off the canister, dropping it with a clang. Griffin held his breath when the Mentor straightened up, his eyes narrowed.

"What did you just say?"

"Nothing," Sergei grunted as he dumped the used grounds in the trash, then scooped fresh beans into the machine.

Oh, wrong answer, dude, Griffin thought. He settled back to enjoy the fireworks. While he watched, Basil started to speak, then paused.

"Fin, go take your shower."

"But I haven't had breakfast yet."

"You can eat afterwards. Go."

Taking his mug with him, Griffin wandered out of the kitchen toward the stairs, stalling. *I know how that conversation's going to go down,* he thought, loitering in the living room; he picked up his pace at a sharp command from Basil. Reaching his room, he dug through his dresser and pulled out clean clothes, then slipped into the bathroom. After a quick shower, he dressed and left. While he tidied his bed, he heard Sergei stomp into his room and shut the door. Hard.

Griffin grinned and punched his fist into the air.

***

"So did Sergei get into trouble?" asked Katie as they walked down the street, her nose pink from the cold. They turned the corner and angled through the park, heading for downtown. She tucked a mittened hand into his.

"Big time," Griffin said. "He thinks he's so—"

A cry of rage shattered the midday calm. They stopped in confusion. Cruel laughter echoed from behind a row of bushes edging the park.

"What the heck?" Griffin craned his neck. He took a step, then another, then broke into a sprint at a second shriek, Katie on his heels.

They crashed through the vegetation, the bare branches tearing at them, and burst out along the bank of a shallow creek. Before they could stop him, a boy shoved a younger one into the stream. The child tripped over a half-submerged log. He fell with a splash and smacked his knee on a rock; he cried out as he clutched his leg. "I'm telling Mom!" he yelled, tears threatening.

"Go ahead. I'll just tell her you fell in when you were messing around." He laughed in his younger brother's face.

"Why, you little bully!"

The boy spun around at the shout of outrage. Before Griffin could catch him, he dashed away and disappeared around the bend.

Griffin started after him, then stopped himself. Basil's voice rang in his head. *Remember, Tiro, we are more Red Cross than Special Forces. Our mandate does not include chasing down the 'bad guys' but rather helping the victims.* He groaned in frustration and turned back.

The little boy hobbled out of the water. Tears of pain and fury streamed down his cheeks.

"Here—let me help you." Griffin took his arm. "No, don't sit down," he added as the boy began to sink to the ground. "We've got to get you home and dry."

Darby Karchut

"M-my knee hurts," the boy gasped. "Really bad." He stood stiffly, arms held away from his body as he shivered, his teeth chattering in a rapid staccato.

While Katie kept a supporting hand on the boy's shoulder, Griffin yanked his hoodie off and wrapped it around the boy. "Do you live close by?"

"A-across the street. The y-yellow house on the corner. But I don't think I can walk." His face crumbled as he sobbed. "I'm cold. I want to go home."

"Katie, go get his mother. Quick." As she sprinted away, he tucked his jacket tighter around the boy. "My girlfriend went to get your mom." Feeling the boy's violent shivers, he glanced across the park and chewed on his lip when he spied Katie only halfway to her destination. He frowned and turned back. "What's your name?"

"Ryan."

"Listen, Ryan. I'm going to give you a piggyback ride home. Okay?"

"Okay."

This way, I can keep him warm at least, he thought. Turning his back on the boy, Griffin squatted down on his heels. "Put your arms around my neck. Tighter. Good. And just let your hurt leg hang down." He slid an arm under the boy's uninjured limb and cautiously stood up. "All set back there?"

"Yeah."

"Here we go." Walking as gently as he could, Griffin clambered up the slope and pushed through the bushes. Twiggy fingers scratched at both of them; Ryan buried his face between Griffin's shoulder blades for protection.

When he cleared the vegetation, Griffin halted and sucked in a deep breath. He tensed his entire body as he struggled to elevate his body temperature. The familiar warmth swelled up in his chest like a balloon, pushing against his ribs and sternum, then radiated outward. The tips of his fingers and toes tingled. *Now if I can just hold it at this level until I get him home. Without passing out.*

Griffin's Fire

Head down in concentration, Griffin started forward. After a few steps, he could hear Ryan weeping again as his soaked jeans and shirt added to his misery. Picking up his pace, Griffin blinked when sweat began trickling down his face; steam rose from their clothing. When he reached the middle of the park, he paused, dizzy from the effort of controlling his Element. *If I push my temp up any more, I'm going to burst into flame.* He hoisted the boy higher on his back. "Halfway there," he wheezed. "You still okay?"

"I guess." Ryan sniffed, wiping his runny nose on the back of Griffin's shirt.

"Gross, dude." He staggered on. Black dots began dancing on the edge of his vision, then he missed a step and stumbled, jostling Ryan's injured leg.

"Ow!"

"Sorry," Griffin gasped. He stopped again, his chest heaving and his pulse roaring in his ears. *Fire, I forgot how hard this was. I must be out of practice.* He looked up and groaned with relief at the sight of Katie racing back across the street. A woman with a blanket under one arm followed close behind.

"Hey, here comes your mom." Griffin crouched down, his legs trembling, and slid Ryan off his back. Keeping an arm around the boy, he slumped to the ground, panting as he pushed his soaked hair off his forehead. He grinned at Katie as she arrived first. Before he could speak, the mother rushed up.

"Ryan! What on earth?" She shook out the blanket and tucked it around the boy, then tugged up his pant leg and examined his knee. Gathering her son into her arms, she looked over at Griffin and Katie. "I don't know how to thank you for this."

"Um...can I have my hoodie back?"

Katie reached over and unwound it from Ryan. With a final word of gratitude, the woman hurried away, the boy waving back at them over her shoulder.

Darby Karchut

"I hope that older brother gets it from his mom. Boys are so mean," Katie said, waving back. "Always punching and shoving each other."

"And girls aren't just as cruel?" Griffin tugged his hoodie back on, grateful for its refreshing dampness.

"Sure we are. Except instead of hitting, we give each other eating disorders." She glanced down at him. "Why are you still sitting there?"

"Just resting—that kid weighed a lot, you know."

"Yeah, right." She held out a hand and pulled him to his feet. "Come on—the movie starts at twelve-fifteen and I want to get there early. I'm in a serious popcorn and Milk Duds mood."

Ten minutes into the film, Katie glanced over as she pried the last piece of candy out of the box and popped it into her mouth. She grinned at the sight of Griffin sprawled in his seat, his head lolling against the backrest and his mouth sagging open.

Sound asleep.

Chapter Nineteen

Basil's Journal: Saturday, January 22nd

I'm not sure who is more difficult to live with: a teenager with self-esteem issues or an apprentice who thinks he's one of God's gifts to the world. Literally.

Besides some rather rude behavior at breakfast, Sergei also made a remark which earned him a dressing down, as well as extra chores for a week. He told me quite bluntly Griffin was an embarrassment to Terrae Angeli everywhere, and since he did not have anything better to do in his free time, why can't he do all the chores around the house?

I'm afraid I didn't handle the situation very well. Perhaps I am overly-protective of the lad, but I will not stand for Sergei's elitist attitude. I made it abundantly clear that all three of us are equal members of this household.

Griffin's Journal: Saturday, January 22nd

I had a mission today! Well, not really a mission. It was more I just helped someone. But I got to use my Fire. In a way.

I better start doing some of those drills Basil used to make me do when I was a kid. Just to keep my skills up. Not to mention my endurance. I fell asleep and missed the entire movie! (No loss there—I'm not that much into fantasy. More of a sci-fi fan.) Katie teased me all the way home about it. After eating an entire box of Milk Duds! I'm surprised she could talk with her teeth stuck together.

The Heflins are coming for dinner. To meet Sergei.

Wow. Lucky them.

He is so pissed off right now. Basil made him straighten up the house and clean the kitchen for being rude at breakfast. He even has to set the table for tonight. I don't have to do one thing. Maybe he'll stop being such a Ser-jerk now.

But I doubt it.

* * *

"Katie, take the casserole over since you've got your jacket on." Helen gestured toward the covered dish steaming on top of the stove. "Tell Mr. Raine that we'll be along in a few minutes." She headed for the stairs. "And use some oven mitts. It's hot."

Katie grumbled under her breath. *I look like a lobster in these things*, she thought as she slid on the red-checkered mitts. She opened and closed them like claws, and then picked up the dish. A whine caught her attention. Bear gazed at her from his dog bed in the corner, his tail thumping hopefully. "Not this time, big guy. Sorry." She headed out of the kitchen and down the hall. Juggling the dish in one hand, she opened the door and eased out, pulling it closed with her foot.

Careful of the icy patches, Katie made her way across the street as the zesty aroma of herbs and cheese rose from the dish in her hands. Out of habit, she glanced up at Griffin's window. She grinned when she saw him wave, and then disappear. As she climbed their porch steps, the door opened.

"Let me get that for you," Griffin said as he stepped outside. Before she could stop him, he took the casserole dish in his bare hands.

Katie gasped. "Griffin—no." She snatched it back, almost dropping it. "Are you crazy? Did you burn yourself?"

"Of course not. I—" His eyes opened wide. "Oh, I mean, yes. Wow, that thing's really hot." He blew on his hands. "What was I thinking?"

"Apparently, you weren't. Here—hang on a sec." She juggled the mitts and dish, then passed them to him. Putting a hand on his back, she steered him inside. "Go on. I'll get the door." As they headed down the hall, Sergei stepped out of the study behind them.

"Well, hello. You must be Katie Heflin." They turned as he swaggered toward them, squaring his shoulders. A twinge of jealously shot through Griffin in a green flash. Before he could make introductions, Sergei held out his hand. "I'm Sergei, Tiro to Mentor Basil."

"Nice to meet you." Katie shook his hand.

"May I help you with your coat?" Without waiting for an answer, he moved behind her and slid her jacket off her shoulders with a flourish.

As Sergei stepped away to hang it on a coat hook, Katie caught Griffin's eye. To his relief, she made a gagging motion. He smiled back and gestured with his head toward the living room. Before Sergei noticed, they darted through the archway and across the living room, escaping to the kitchen.

"Hi, Mr. Raine." Katie grabbed a carrot off the snack tray as she took a seat at the table.

"Hello, Katie. And when are you going to start addressing me as Basil?" he asked with a smile as he motioned for Griffin to place the casserole on top of the stove.

"When I'm twenty-one. Or get a new set of parents. They'll be over in a minute, by the way."

"Right. You two keep an eye on things while I run upstairs, eh?" He hurried out of the room.

Griffin took a seat next to Katie and held out the oven mitts. Flexing his arms and sticking out his chest, he deepened his voice in mockery. "May I help you on with these?" They swallowed their laughter when Sergei walked in.

Darby Karchut

The Tiro narrowed his eyes as he studied their faces, and then opened a drawer and scooped up the silverware. After slamming the drawer closed with a hip, he turned and stomped back out.

They watched him leave, then grinned at each other and bumped fists.

Katie's Journal: Saturday, January 22nd

We had dinner with the Raines this evening. Griffin was right. Sergei sure thinks the world of himself. He kept flirting with me the entire meal. Other girls might be impressed with his smooth moves, but I'm not. (He is good looking, though. I mean, really, really good looking. Must be a Terrae Angelus thing.)

Mom and Dad were polite to him. Dad asked him some questions, but mostly they talked with Basil. Of course, Griffin and I made fun of him when no one was looking.

Later, when I told Mom my opinion of Sergei, she reminded me that I need to remember he might be having a hard time, too. That he is probably missing his Mentor and feeling like the outsider.

I hate it when she makes me look at the other person's point of view.

Chapter Twenty

The receptionist looked up at the two men striding toward her across the hotel lobby. She fixed a trained smile on her face and nodded. "Hello, gentlemen. Welcome to the Broadmoor."

"Good afternoon, miss," said the taller of the two, his white hair brilliant in the light from the crystal chandelier hanging from the flamboyant ceiling. "We're attempting to locate a friend of ours."

"Going to play some golf with him," the second man added, running a heavy hand along the carved edge of the counter. The receptionist open and closed her mouth as she took in his cowboy boots and fringed, leather jacket. He stared back, his black eyes wide with mock innocence. "What?"

Basil cleared his throat. "Sukalli, please." He nudged the Guardian to one side. "Our friend may be registered under the name Nicopolis. He probably checked in within the last few weeks or so. Would you be able to help us?"

As the woman bent over her keyboard, Basil turned to Sukalli and spoke in a low voice. "It's doubtful he would have used his real name, but one never knows."

"Well, Nan-ja and her Tiro only caught a glimpse, but she was sure it was him." Sukalli snorted as he glanced around. "Only Nicopolis would hide out at a five star resort."

"I'm sorry, sir," the receptionist said after a few minutes, "but we have no guest with that name."

Before Basil could press for more information, Sukalli elbowed him into silence. "Thanks anyway, missy," he said and motioned for Basil to follow him across the lobby. Disregarding the escalator, they jogged up the marble stairs to the main lounge. A wall of glass framed the view of a sweeping patio bordering the man-made lake as well as the mountains rising in the west.

"Thought we just take a look around ourselves and see if we can spot him." Sukalli pushed through the heavy glass door and headed north along the walkway encircling the water. "Or smell him."

"Smell him? I thought you considered him a snake."

"Nope. Changed it to skunk."

Basil shook his head in amusement, glad for the presence of the other Terrae Angelus at his side. "I doubt he will be eager to accompany us back to the Foundation."

"Oh, he may buck, but he's no match for a double dose of Might. That's why I'm along." Sukalli snapped his fingers. Flames skipped along their tips. With a grin, he held them up and blew them out like candles on a birthday cake.

A memory washed over Basil, more poignant than painful. Of a fourteen year old Griffin, all legs and feet from a sudden growth spurt, sprawled on the sofa and watching the television. Flicking his thumb like a Zippo lighter as he ignited the end of it. Over and over until Basil was ready to yell. Then sputtering with laughter when his Mentor finally sprayed a jet of Water at him in desperation.

Basil tightened his lips and wrenched his focus back on the present. "Promise me you will be discreet. The last thing we need is a battle in public."

Sukalli gave him a curious look. "That goes for you, too, brother."

"What are you implying?"

"Look, you've got a pile of righteous anger steaming inside of you over what Nicopolis did to Griffin. And I know you. You are slow to anger, but once you go into avenging angel mode, there's no reining you back."

"I have no idea what you're talking about." Basil kept his eyes fixed ahead. Sukalli snorted in disbelief.

They continued walking, scanning the area. Leaving the busy patio behind, they passed a more secluded wing of the hotel tucked amongst towering pines. A side door swung open into their path.

Nicopolis stepped out. Humming to himself, he straightened his tie, then smoothed his thin hair across his brow. He glanced around. The color drained from his face when he spotted them.

Basil leaped forward, Sukalli a split second behind him. They each grabbed an arm and hustled Nicopolis backwards until all three were hidden inside a grove of trees. As Nicopolis started to protest, Sukalli clapped a hand over his mouth.

"Save it for the judge." Sukalli tightened his grip on the struggling Nicopolis. "You ready?" he asked Basil.

Basil checked over his shoulder, then nodded. "All clear."

In a blast of wind, all three disappeared. Pine needles swirled upward in a mini-tornado before drifting back down.

* * *

Basil leaned against the stone wall of the windowless room and crossed his arms over his chest as he watched. The light from candles mounted in wall sconces flickered over Mayla and Nicopolis sitting face to face in the center of the room. Sukalli waited nearby. The scent of melting wax filled the room.

Mayla tightened her grip on Nicopolis' hands. The Mentor swayed in his chair, his mouth hanging slack. After a few minutes, she let go with a sigh. Nicopolis continued to sit motionless, his pale eyes blank as he stared into space.

"Not only did Griffin pass his *Proelium*," she said, "he did it quite cleverly, too."

Basil started to speak, then stopped and ran a hand down his face. A white-hot ball of rage swelled in his chest. Fighting to tamp it back down, he pushed away from the wall and walked to the opposite end of the room. "So what happens next?"

"Now it is up to Command to decide his fate." Mayla waved a hand in front of Nicopolis' face and murmured softly. As he blinked and looked around in confusion, she joined Sukalli standing near the door. "We'll leave him here for now until he becomes more alert."

Basil nodded absently, his gaze fixed on Nicopolis. A strange expression clouded his face.

Sukalli watched his old friend for a moment. With a knowing smile, he reached out and took Mayla's elbow. "Why, you must be tired after performing the Search. Let me help you out."

"What in Heaven's name are you talking about? I feel fine..." Her voice trailed off as Sukalli bent down and began whispering in her ear. A smile tugged at the corner of her mouth.

"You are wicked, do you know that, Sukalli?" she murmured. "Pure evil." She stood up. "Why, yes, I *am* rather weary," Mayla announced in a loud voice. "A cup of tea would be lovely." Without another word, they slipped out and closed the door.

Pausing in the hall, they listened as a voice squeaked in fear. The sound of a chair crashing to the floor was followed by a muffled thump, then another. A minute later, the door opened.

Basil stepped out. Massaging his knuckles, he looked from one Guardian to the other, then cleared his throat.

"You might have heard a commotion just now," he said. "I'm afraid I must confess—"

Before Basil could say another word, Mayla turned toward Sukalli. "Did *you* hear anything?"

"You mean besides the sound of Nicopolis *accidentally tripping* over his chair?" Sukalli's smile matched Mayla's. "Nope—didn't hear a thing."

Basil's Journal: Thursday, January 27th

I should feel some remorse about punching Nicopolis in the

face. Perhaps one day I will. (But I very much doubt it.)

And so now Command knows. Griffin had passed his *Proelium* and Nicopolis had lied to hurt me by destroying Griffin.

But it gets worse.

In a cruel twist, Command has chosen to simply re-assign Nicopolis to another region, even over the Guardians' fierce objections and my less-than-tactful suggestion what they could do with their decision. Command argued that Nicopolis could still be useful in the field somewhere. Furthermore, they are currently unresolved as to strip him of his rank as a Senior Mentor.

What a complete and utter muck-up.

At least they agreed to keep all this under wraps until I decide if and when to inform Griffin.

So here I sit. Waiting for the dawn. Wondering if I *should* tell him. That it was all a mistake and that the bright future he worked so hard for was taken from him through no fault of his own.

God help me, but I can't do it. I can't break his heart again.

Maybe one day he'll know the truth.

Chapter Twenty-One

Griffin's Journal: Tuesday, February 1st
I'm fried.

I've been doing drills and exercises at night whenever I can sneak past everyone. Since I can't go on missions, this is the only way I know to stay sharp. The problem is I'm not getting my homework done and my teachers are getting pissed. Hope they don't call Basil.

My Elements are almost back to the level they were in December, but my use of Might is still hit-or-miss (nothing new there–I've always had problems with it. Basil once told me that a lot of Terrae Angeli have trouble using Might, not just apprentices) and I'm screwing up on short flights. I think I'm taking off too hard, but I don't know how to fix it.

Basil would know.

I wish it were Saturday. I'm starting to hate school. I've overslept a few times and had to walk. So then I'm late to my first class, which means I get detention from Milton after school, so I can't start my homework until I get home, so then I have to stay up late to train AND do my work. And then I end up sleeping through my alarm clock again!!!

The hardest part is keeping it a secret from everyone.

Basil's been acting totally weird lately. For the last week now he's been really quiet. Almost....*sad*. A couple of times, he'd start to tell me something, then stop himself.

I wish I knew what it was.

* * *

Griffin balanced on one bare foot on the wide windowsill of his bedroom. His hand rested on the drapery rod for balance. *Hmmm—maybe if I bend my knees more.* He took a deep breath, then leaped into the air and vanished.

Reappearing across the room, he stumbled and fell to one knee with a thump. *Fire, I keep screwing up the landing.* Hitching up his sweatpants, he hurried around his bed and clambered back up. He launched himself again, this time tripping over his desk chair as he materialized. Swearing from a stubbed toe, he limped back over to the window. He hoisted himself up on the ledge, paused for a moment, then tried again.

The bathroom door rolled open with a rumble. Sergei walked in.

Griffin reappeared in midair. He dove for his bed and landed in an awkward belly flop, the mattress springs protesting with a squeal. Panting, he raised his face.

Sergei slouched in the doorway, a knowing look on his face. "Oh, I can't wait to tell Basil about *this*."

Griffin rolled off his bed and wiped his face with his tee shirt. "About what?"

"About what you were doing just now."

"What do you mean?" Panic worms began squirming in his stomach.

"I mean you jumping on the bed. Like some dorky kid."

Griffin sank back down on the edge of the mattress, his legs flimsy with relief. "Go ahead and tell him," he said, hoping Sergei didn't catch the faint quiver in his voice. "He won't care." *That was too close—I have got to be more careful. The guy would wet himself with excitement if he got the chance to tell on me.*

"Oh, right. Because you're *special*. Basil's little charity case."

"Jealous?"

"Of you?" Sergei sneered. "Why would I be jealous of a Lucy?" He straightened up, flexing his shoulders as he stretched his arms over his head and hooked his fingers on the top of the doorframe. "I passed *my Proelium* in three minutes. Didn't even bother to take off my jacket."

"Four is what Basil told me."

"Whatever. At least I passed and in the fastest time ever. Of course, my Mentor always told me I would probably break the record."

"Yet he dumped you the first chance he got to go on a long-term mission. I wonder why?"

Sergei dropped his arms, his face flush with anger, and for a fleeting moment, hurt. "He *had* to go. Dimitri's an expert on that region and they needed him. Thousands of lives were at stake or he wouldn't have left me."

"You're kind of touchy about that. Did I hit a nerve?" Before Sergei could respond, Griffin walked over to his desk and yanked out the chair. "I've got work to do." He flipped through a folder and removed a worksheet. "Which means go away." He gritted his teeth when Sergei ignored the request and strolled into the room.

Throwing himself down on the bed, Sergei leaned back on one elbow, jiggling his foot. "So how long have you known Katie?"

"About five months." Griffin turned his back on him and dug in his drawer for his calculator.

"And what's her preference? Now that she's had a sample of both—human or angel?"

"What?" Griffin spun around. "Are you—"

"You can't blame me. She's hot. And with her looks, she could pass for a Terrae Angelus. In fact, *we* would make a perfect couple, don't you think?" He sat up and laughed as Griffin swelled with rage.

"Leave her alone! Katie's my—"

"Oh, get over yourself. Like I would ever actually date a mortal. Unlike some, I know better than to mix with humans on a social level." He stood up. "Of course, in Katie's case, I'd make an exception," he said over his shoulder as he sauntered back to his bedroom. The door banged closed behind him.

Griffin threw his pencil across the room. Cursing under his breath, he used every word Basil forbade him to say. After a solid minute of trash-mouth therapy, he scrubbed his face with both hands and glanced down at his homework. *I'm never going to be able to concentrate now, thanks to Ser-jerk. I guess I'll go work out and then tackle this again later.*

He dressed quickly, then closed his door behind him. With shoes in hand, he crept downstairs to the kitchen. He paused and checked his watch. *Let's see—it's seven thirty. Basil said he'll be home no later than eleven, so I should have plenty of time to train and finish my homework.* Easing out the door, he stopped to pull on his shoes, and then raced across the yard toward the back wall. He vanished after a few strides.

Griffin reappeared in the dark field beyond on steady legs. *Now why can't I stick the landing* inside *the house?* He shook his head and looked around to check the adjacent backyards, then walked to the middle of the empty lot. The glow of the downtown lights illuminated the bellies of the clouds overhead. *Looks like it's going to snow tonight*, he thought, sniffing at the dampness in the air. *Good. Then I don't have to bury the ashes afterwards.* With a final glance at the sky, he began.

Taking a deep breath, he closed his eyes. A smile crept across his face as he remembered the first time Basil had explained the reason for all their drills and exercises.

Just like humans, my young Tiro, we also must keep in top form. For it is through the merging of our physical bodies with our elemental powers that we can achieve our highest and best reason for existence. And what do you think that reason would be?

To kick butt?

Tempting to do so in certain occasions, but no. Think again.

To help others?

Aye, lad, to help others.

Darby Karchut

True that, Griffin thought. He stretched his arms out on either side. Flames erupted from his fingertips. Crouching slightly, he spun on his toes. Fire streamed down and outward, melting snow and charring clumps of winter grass in a perfect arc around him. He leaped up, landed a few yards away, and ignited his Fire again, torching a second ring. Over and over, he repeated the ancient movements, lost in the rhythm as he created a series of overlapping circles across the field.

When he finished the last one an hour later, he staggered to a stop, his arms cramping from the effort and his hoodie stained with sweat. *I wish I could use my Elements* during *flight. It sure would be a lot easier than having to turn them on and off.* Clasping his hands on top of his head, he walked around as he cooled off and examined his handiwork. *And people always think those circles were made by UFOs.*

Something cold brushed his cheek. As he looked up, heavy snowflakes began falling. *Perfect! They'll cover my marks.*

He jogged home, vaulted the stone wall and hurried on to the kitchen door. Slipping inside, he toed off his shoes and padded across the house and up the stairs. He paused at the sight of a note stuck to his closed door. *Out on a mission - S.*

Good. Stay gone.

Grabbing the paper, he crumbled it up as he stepped inside. He pulled off his hoodie. After draping it over his chair to dry, he picked up his math book and flopped stomach-down on the bed. With a sigh, he started on the first problem.

An hour later, Griffin jerked awake when a hand shook his shoulder. "Are we on call?" he mumbled as he lifted his head and peeled the worksheet off his cheek, the pencil still clasped in his hand. He felt the mattress sag.

"No, lad," Basil replied, taking a seat. "Say, where's Sergei?"

Griffin rolled over, bleary-eyed. "On a mission." He yawned, then sat up, wiping the trickle of drool off the corner of his mouth. "Right."

Griffin's Fire

Glancing in surprise at Griffin's homework assignment, Basil picked it up with a huff of exasperation at the mostly empty page. He shifted on the bed, the paper still in his hand, then stopped and frowned. He sniffed at Griffin, and then leaned closer and sniffed again.

"What?" Griffin blinked in confusion.

Basil started to speak, then shook his head. "Nothing." He waved the paper like a warning flag. "Procrastinating again?"

With a shrug, Griffin took the worksheet back. "No more than usual." He peered up at Basil's face. "Hey, are you okay?"

"I'm fine. Just a bit weary. It was a difficult mission."

"Successful?"

"Sadly, no." Basil stood up, checking the clock by the bed as he headed toward the door. "Best finish your assignment. You wouldn't want another detention from Mr. Milton, eh?"

"You know about those?"

"He rang up me last week. After you earned a third one for incomplete work as well as being tardy. He was rather...blunt...about it."

Blunt is not the word I would have used, Griffin thought. "Uh... not that I'm looking for trouble, but why didn't you yell at me or ground me or something?"

Basil kneaded the back of his neck. "Do I need to?"

"No, sir."

"Are you going to be more diligent about your schooling?" He dropped his hand and stared at Griffin.

"Yes, sir."

"I assume I won't be hearing from the gentleman again?"

"No, sir."

"Then consider yourself properly chastised. Now finish up and then bed." He smiled wearily as he closed the door.

Darby Karchut

Griffin stared into space as he listened to Basil's footsteps fadingaway. He looked down at his homework, then nodded to himself. Stretching across the bed, he grabbed the alarm off his nightstand, punched the volume to maximum, and set it on his desk.

Basil's Journal: Wednesday, February 2nd

Bloody horrible day! A failed mission and I am uneasy about Griffin. He's not at all himself these days. Well, his *new* self, that is. He appears exhausted all the time and his school performance is slipping. And tonight I thought I smelled a trace of smoke on his clothes, but I couldn't be sure.

Now where would he get cigarettes?

Griffin's Journal: Wednesday, February 2nd

Good practice session this evening, but too close a call. Sergei walked in on me right in the middle of a flight. I almost broke my neck diving for my bed at the last second. Luckily, he thought I was just messing around. Like a sixteen year old guy would have nothing better to do than jump on his bed! Talk about clueless! He was being a jerk about Katie. Of course, he's a jerk about everything.

But it's Basil that worries me more than Sergei. Nothing, and I do mean NOTHING, ever gets past him. I think he smelled smoke on my clothes, but he didn't ask me about it. He was more concerned that I was behind on my homework. I have got to figure out a way to juggle everything so he doesn't get suspicious.

It's after eleven and I'm still stuck on two problems. Maybe Katie can help me before school.

Chapter Twenty-Two

"See? You have to do it for both sides of the equation." Katie leaned against Griffin's shoulder as she circled the problem, then handed him the pencil. "Here—try the next one."

"Okay."

While he worked, she glanced around the library. "Look at all those posters about the Valentine dance. They must have put one up on every square foot of the whole school." She studied his profile as he bent over the paper. "Yup. Lots of posters. About the dance. The *Valentine* dance." She waited hopefully for a moment. "It's on Friday the eleventh," she added. "I heard they're going to have a decent band, too. You know—at the *dance*. The Valentine dance. Next Friday. Here at school."

He nodded absently and scribbled the next answer. "Is this right?" He slid the paper over to her.

Katie sighed in resignation as she looked it over. "You got it." She smiled at his irresistible grin and squeezed his arm. "We'll make a math whiz out of you yet."

"What, and deny Milton the pleasure of flunking me?" he said, standing up and shoving his materials in his book bag. He hooked the strap over his shoulder, then checked his watch. "Speaking of the devil, I better go. The guy's a tyrant about being to class on time."

After walking Katie to her locker, Griffin headed around the corner. He nodded hello to several classmates and took a position near the closed door. Leaning back with one foot braced on the wall behind him, he waited with the others. Their conversation flowed around him.

"If I get one more detention, my mom is going to take away my cell," said a nearby girl to her friend.

Her friend snorted. "Yeah, well. If I don't keep a B average, then I can't go out with Mitch anymore." They glanced over at Griffin, then leaned their heads together and whispered for a moment. Her friend nodded, and then whispered back. "So go ask him. What do you got to lose? At least he'll know you're interested in him."

The first girl nodded and tugged at her low cut tee. She flipped her long hair around one shoulder. Sliding nearer, she smiled up at him as she leaned a hip against the wall. "Hi, Griffin."

"Hey, Stephanie. How's it going?" He found himself staring at her shirt for a moment before wrenching his eyes up to her face.

"So, did you understand the homework?" she asked. "I was really stuck on the last two problems."

Finding his gaze sneaking downward again, Griffin mentally socked himself in the jaw. "Yeah, me too. I had to get some help on it this morning." He straightened up, grateful to be moving, and pulled his book bag around. "Do you want to see what I got for the answers? I can show you—"

"Oh, no, I'm good. But thanks—you're sweet to offer." She beamed at him, tilting her head to one side. She leaned closer to talk as students began filling the hall. "Actually, I was wondering if you were planning on going to the school's Valentine dance next Friday."

Griffin's heart skipped a beat. "I-I didn't know about it." *Was I supposed to ask Katie? I wish she would've given me some kind of hint.* "So this dance—it's here at school?"

The girl blinked in surprise. "Well, yeah. That's why it's called a *school* dance."

"Next Friday?"

"Uh-huh."

Griffin's Fire

"And it's in honor of St. Valentine, but it's not *on* St. Valentine's Day?"

"Well, no."

Okay, I am so not getting this. He glanced at his watch. "Excuse me. I need to do something before class." Hitching his bag higher on his shoulder, he rushed away, zigzagging through the growing crowd. Halfway down the hall, a hand smacked him on the back.

"Hey, Griffin." Cas fell into step beside him. "Still want to work on our presentation after school? We can catch a ride home with my dad if you don't mind waiting around. He said it'd be about forty-five minutes."

"Yeah, that'd be fine. Listen, I'm in a hurry—"

"Dude, restrooms are the other way." Cas peeled off with a wave.

Sliding to a stop by Katie's English class, Griffin ducked in the door and scanned the milling group. He finally spotted her sitting on top of a desk chatting with another girl while they waited for the teacher. "Katie!"

Her head whipped around, her eyes widening with alarm; she hopped off and rushed over. "What wrong?" she asked, grabbing his arm.

"Oh, nothing. Nothing's wrong—I just need to ask you something." He cocked his head. "Outside?" Taking her elbow, he ushered her through the door. As the hall emptied around them, he checked the wall clock and clasped both her hands. "Look, I'm sorry. Was I supposed to ask you to the dance? Because I just found out about it."

"Calm down." Katie squeezed his fingers. "I was going to talk with you at lunch." She laughed at his relieved expression, and then jumped when her teacher marched past them into the room.

"Get to class, you two," she said over her shoulder. "Or you're both going to be tardy."

Darby Karchut

"So what do I—" Griffin started to speak when Katie gave him a shove.

"Go! We'll talk about it later!"

As Katie ducked inside, Griffin ran back down the empty corridor, his footsteps echoing against the lockers. He flew around the corner to his classroom. As his foot crossed the threshold, the bell rang. Panting, he stopped and peered through the doorway.

Milton sat perched on his tall chair in front of the class, the ever-constant mug in one hand. He looked over when Griffin slipped inside. "Oh, no you don't," he said as Griffin started toward the back of the room. "You just stand right there, Raine with-an-e." He swept an arm around in a broad gesture. "Here's an example of someone who thinks the rules don't apply to him," he announced to the class. He took a sip as he stared at Griffin. "By the way, I called your dad last week. About your detentions and your late assignments."

"I know. He told me."

"Yeah, I can see that was a waste of my time. I figured from his accent that you're a real daddy's boy. What did he do to you anyway? Make you skip afternoon tea and crumpets one day?"

The class laughed. Fury mixed with embarrassment flooded Griffin; he tried to ignore the blur of faces and whispering voices. *And I promised him just last night that I wouldn't get in trouble again.* The image of Basil's exhausted face floated through his mind. For a fleeting moment, Griffin saw him not as the all-powerful Mentor, but simply as another being. With burdens of his own. *And all I'm doing is adding to them.* His face reddened.

Enjoying Griffin's humiliation, Milton took a few more leisurely sips, then turned to the class. "All right. The rest of you, open to page sixty-six and do the odd numbered problems. And I don't want to hear a sound until I get back." He put the mug on his desk behind him, then heaved himself up and walked over. "Okay, Raine. Out in the hall."

"Mr. Milton, I'm sorry—" he began when the teacher slammed the door behind them, rattling the nearby lockers.

Griffin's Fire

"Shut your mouth and stand against the wall." Milton waited until Griffin backed up a step. Shaking his gray mane out of his eyes, he stepped closer. "You don't seem to get it, do you? In here, you play by *my* rules." He stabbed his finger into Griffin's chest.

Griffin's eyes flashed with brown fire. *Touch me again and I'll break it off.*

"Half hour detention. Today after school."

"I can't. I have to—"

"For disrupting class and mouthing off to me. Keep arguing and I'll make an hour." Griffin clamped his mouth closed. "Good boy." Milton jerked his head toward the door. "Now get your butt in there and get to work."

After his last class, Griffin dragged himself back to Milton's room. The teacher pointed to a desk in the front row. Without a word, he took a seat.

He glanced up as Milton dialed the phone, battering the numbers with a heavy hand. Cradling the receiver between his jaw and shoulder, he picked up his clipboard and scribbled on it.

"Let's see what daddy has to say this time." He rocked back in his chair as he spoke, his eyes fixed on Griffin. "Mr. Raine? Milton here from the high school. We spoke last week about your kid. I wanted to let you know he was late again this morning and gave me lip about it. You know, you might try using some discipline at home because...what's that? Oh, sure. He's sitting right here." Milton waved Griffin over and handed him the receiver with a smirk.

Turning his back on the teacher, Griffin stepped as far away as the cord allowed. "Hey, it's me."

"Tell me you were buried in an avalanche and had to dig your way out, thus causing you to be delayed," Basil said, his voice sharp with irritation.

"Uh...no, sir."

"Katie?"

"Yes, sir."

"*She* was buried in an avalanche?"

Darby Karchut

"No, sir."

His heart began to sink as Basil let out a long sigh. "You do realize that your behavior reflects not only on you, but also upon me and *my* guidance."

Griffin's heart went into free fall and crashed somewhere around his toes.

* * *

"Thanks again for waiting," Griffin said to Cas.

"No problem. Dad was running late anyway. Here, check this idea out." Cas pulled several sheets out of the printer on his desk. He swiveled around and handed them to Griffin sitting crossed-legged on the bedroom floor, a bowl of popcorn in his lap. The aroma of overheated imitation butter filled the room.

Griffin wiped his fingers on his jeans, then grabbed the papers and shuffled through them. "So do like a timeline?"

"It'd be a lot more interesting than—" Cas stopped and looked past Griffin at his open door. "Tessie, no. Quit bugging us. Man, she does this every time you come over."

"I don't mind." Griffin grinned as the little girl danced in and flung herself onto his back. She wrapped her tiny arms around his neck. "Gwiffin, Gwiffin," she crooned, bouncing up and down. Her bare toes slipped on his tee shirt as she tried to climb up.

"You can have her." Leaning over, Cas grabbed a few kernels and waved them at his sister. "Tessie, want some popcorn?" When she nodded, he threw them out the door into the hallway. "Go get em!"

"Dude, she's not a dog," Griffin said in amusement as Tessie slid down and trotted toward the snacks. He rolled over and snagged the hem of her jumper just in time. "And anyway, your mom wants us to watch her until she gets back with the pizza." He reeled the child back in while Tessie shrieked with laughter.

"You sure you don't want her?"

"We're running out of room as it is."

"How's it going with your cousin? Any better?"

"Are you kidding?" Griffin made a face, then brightened. "Hey, I'll trade you Tessie for Ser-jerk."

They both laughed at the nickname, then Cas shook his head. "I guess I'm stuck with her." He stood up. "I'll get us some sodas. Be right back."

As Griffin started to reach for more popcorn, Tessie twisted around and peered into his face, her eyes wide with curiosity. "Gwiffin, where's wings?" She patted one of his shoulder blades with her tiny hand. "Wings gone?"

"No wings, Tessie. Not that kind of angel." He chuckled as she flung her arms out and scampered in a circle around him.

"Me can fly," she crowed. She made another loop, almost putting her foot into the bowl, and then veered out the door and down the hall, flapping madly.

Griffin scrambled to his feet. *I better make sure she isn't heading for the stairs.* As he stepped into the hallway, he froze. "Tessie, no!"

Tessie balanced on the top step, twirling on her bare toes, her arms spread wide. "Watch me, Gwiffin. 'Kay? Watch me." Before he could move, she pirouetted once more. Her foot slipped off the tread and she tumbled backwards, her eyes and mouth stretched with fear.

Without thinking, Griffin dove for her. The family photos lining the wall clattered wildly when he blasted past them. Air whistled in his ears as he flew. Stretching full out, he scooped her up before she struck the next tread. He pulled her close and spun around, cradling her with his body, her weight hampering his flight.

They fell.

Griffin landed with a thud. The back of his head smacked against the tile floor. For several minutes, he laid there, opening and closing his mouth like a stranded fish. Tessie laid sprawled on his chest, too stunned to cry.

Darby Karchut

Finally, Griffin managed to suck in a breath. "You okay?" he rasped.

In response, Tessie sat up. Pointing her chin to the ceiling, she burst into tears.

* * *

Gunning the engine of the Saab, Basil spun the steering wheel and sent the sports car into a controlled sideways slide around the corner. With a deft hand, he straightened it, then roared down the street, mailboxes racing past him. Another twist of the wheel, and the car flew into the Navarre's driveway. He stomped on the brakes, leaped out, and sprinted up the walk. The front door opened. Light spilled out as he reached the entry.

"He's fine," James Navarre said as he ushered Basil inside. "Just a bump on the head and a few bruises."

"Right." Basil nodded, taking a deep breath. "And was your daughter injured?" he asked while he followed the man through the house.

"No, thanks to your son. She was more frightened than anything else. I'm still not sure how he did it." He waved Basil into the family room. "I'll get my wife. She's busy raking Cas over the coals for not putting up the safety gate."

Basil paused in the doorway, relief flooding through him. Griffin sat perched on the edge of the sofa, staring at the floor while he held an ice pack against the back of his head. He glanced up and smiled sheepishly.

"Sorry."

"For what—doing the right thing?" Basil joined him. He leaned closer and pulled Griffin's hand away. "Here. Let me see." Examining the bump, he spoke softly. "You saw the little one in danger and you just couldn't help yourself, eh?"

"Yeah. Pretty dumb move."

Griffin's Fire

"Only one of many." He smiled at Griffin's huff of exasperation, and then turned when Mr. and Mrs. Navarre walked in, Tessie dozing in her father's arms. Rising to his feet, he held out a hand. "Mrs. Navarre? I'm Basil Raine."

"Hello, Mr. Raine." She nodded toward Griffin. "I've examined him and he seems okay. No signs of a concussion yet, but you'll want to keep a close eye on him for the next few hours. Uneven or dilated pupils, vomiting, the usual symptoms."

"Sylvia's a trauma nurse," James said. He hefted Tessie more securely in his arms, her face pillowed on his shoulder.

"I will. And please, call me Basil." He smiled when Tessie opened her eyes and lifted her head to gaze at him in astonishment. She stared back and forth between Griffin and Basil.

"Angels," she whispered. She blinked and laid her head down. Her thumb slid into her mouth.

James patted her back. "Thank you, again, for what you did," he said, shaking Griffin's hand. "It was a wonder you caught her."

For a moment, the familiar warmth swelled Griffin's heart. *It's what I do*, he thought. *It's what I should do. Even if nobody ever knows.*

Walking down the driveway through the first flakes of another storm, he rolled his eyes at Basil's supporting grip on his elbow. The Mentor cleared his throat when they reached the car.

"I thought we'd swing by the emergency room. Simply as a precaution."

Griffin stopped and squared his shoulders, the snow beginning to dust his dark hair. "No. No hospital." He held up a hand as Basil started to speak. "Please, let me say something."

Looking his Mentor straight in the eye, Griffin began. "Basil, I know I don't heal as fast as I used to. But I do know how to take a fall. And hold my own in a fight. And help others when I can. Because of what you taught me. So no coddling just because I'm mortal, okay?" He thumped his chest and grinned. "I'm tougher than I look."

Darby Karchut

Basil gazed at him for a moment, then smiled back. "And not just on the outside, lad."

Basil's Journal: Thursday, February 3rd

Not only did Griffin receive another detention from his math instructor this morning (and thus earning snow shoveling duty for a week as a consequence from me), he also tumbled down the stairs saving little Tessie Navarre this afternoon. He has a lump on his head and a bruised back.

And Sergei gashed his hand this evening helping a young lady change a flat tire in the midst of this growing storm. He required six stitches, provided by yours truly.

If *I* survive Griffin's adolescence and Sergei's apprenticeship, it will be a twenty-first century miracle.

Griffin's Journal: Thursday, February 3rd

I wish I could talk to Basil. Yeah, it worked out with Tessie and all, but I sure could use his advice. We used to debrief after each mission. What went right. What went wrong. What I need to work on. Now I'm just guessing.

Maybe I can't do this. At least not on my own.

I re-read my copy of the Kellsfarne. And even tried to do an Internet search. I wish I could figure out how I became an angel again. It wasn't like a bolt of lightning just hit me one day. It was more like my mortality faded away.

Or like the sun rising. A gradual brightening of the day.

Oh, and Ser-Jerk got hurt.

Chapter Twenty-Three

Griffin whimpered at the first beep of the alarm; the shrill sound set his teeth on edge. He poked an arm out from under the quilt, his face still buried in the pillow, and slapped at it. He finally silenced the vile thing. Before he could crawl out of bed, the door opened.

"Fin?" Basil stuck his head inside.

"I know, I know. I'm hurrying." He rolled over and sat up, pushing the covers away.

"No need. Your school has been canceled due to the storm."

Griffin groaned with delight and slumped back over, curling up on his side. "Father in Heaven," he mumbled into the bedding. "We heartily thank you for snow days. Amen."

"Well, before you get too comfortable, remember that you have shovel duty."

"Can I do it after breakfast?"

"No. And I want you to go over and clean the Heflin driveway for Lewis before you tackle ours."

Why don't I just do the entire bloody street? Griffin thought as he sat back up. He glowered at Basil who grinned back and left. He dragged himself out of bed, pulled on some clothes, and headed outside.

After twenty minutes of less than enthusiastic shoveling, Griffin blew his damp hair out of his eyes, panting from exertion. *That's good enough*, he thought, examining both driveways as snow began falling again. *If Basil wants it done better, he can do it himself.*

Leaning the shovel against the side of the garage, he patted his stomach as it gave a growl, then hurried inside for breakfast. After kicking off his boots, he headed across the living room, trying to decide between french toast and waffles. His pace faltered at the sound of laughter coming from the kitchen.

Seated at the cluttered table, Sergei held his palm out to Basil who bent closer and peered at the sutures. Neither of them noticed Griffin in the doorway.

"Then what happened?" Basil asked, fishing through the open first aid kit.

Sergei's eyes danced. "Why, she asked me for my cell phone number, of course." He grinned as Basil shook his head in amusement and applied a clean bandage. "You know how it is for us Wind and Waters."

The corner of Basil's mouth twitched. "I do, indeed."

A green snake twisted around itself in Griffin's chest. Schooling his face, he stalked into the kitchen and made a beeline for the cupboard.

"A bit of a chore, eh, Fin?" Basil said behind him. "With all the snow?"

"Yeah." *Like you care.* As he grabbed a mug, Basil spoke again.

"Sergei, you're off rotation for the next twenty-four hours. And stop scowling—you'll be cleared for duty by tomorrow if that hand heals well enough today."

"But what about you?"

"Oh, I think I can handle a solo mission or two. But if I'm summoned, I need assurance you two will stay out of each other's way."

For a long minute, the only sound was the low moan of the storm outside.

"Gentlemen, I am waiting."

"Fine," Sergei said. He pushed his chair back, the legs screeching along the floor.

Griffin's Fire

"Whatever," Griffin mumbled, staring out the window. Behind him, Basil growled in frustration.

"Sergei, sit back down. No, sit. Griffin, come here."

Turning around, Griffin dragged his feet as he walked over and sank down across the table from Sergei. He pushed the first aid kit to one side, the empty mug still in his hand. "Can I at least get some coffee first?"

"No, you cannot get some bloody coffee first!" Basil took a deep breath, trying to calm himself. Lowering his brows, he fixed an ice-blue gaze on them. "I've had enough of this cold war between the two of you. And I want it to cease. Now."

"Fine."

"Whatever."

"No more provoking each other. No more sniping at one another when my back is turned." His eyes bored into one, than the other. "Do you understand me?"

"Fine."

"Whatever."

Basil sighed and lowered his head, massaging his temples with his fingertips. "By the Light, kill me now."

* * *

Griffin glanced up from the study's sofa as Basil hurried past toward the entryway. Tossing his book aside, he scrambled to his feet and stuck his head out the door. "Got a call?"

Thrusting his arms into his heavy jacket, Basil nodded. "There's a massive pile up on the interstate." He tugged his zipper up to his chin. "Even Sukalli has been summoned." He shot out the front door and disappeared into the storm. "Behave," called a fading voice.

"Yeah, yeah." Griffin began to close the door, then paused at the threshold when he noticed the latest snowfall covering the porch steps. *I probably should clear those again. But then I'd have to go all the way around to the garage for the shovel. And put my boots back on.* He chewed on a thumbnail as he glanced up and down the street at the rest of the neighborhood half hidden by blowing snow. The wind moaned overhead like a lost soul. Coming to a decision, he leaned out the door, stretched out a hand, and aimed downward.

Flames erupted from his fingertips in blazing streamers. *I better be careful I don't set the steps on fire,* he thought as he waved his hand slowly back and forth. The snow hissed as it melted. *I can just see me trying to explain* that *to Basil.* He grinned at the picture.

The whisper of his Fire muted the approaching footsteps behind him.

"What are you doing, Lucy?"

With a yelp of surprise, Griffin snapped his fingers into a fist, extinguishing the flames. He spun around and kicked the door shut with his heel as he faced Sergei. "None of your business." He struggled to keep his face blank.

Sergei elbowed past Griffin, opened the door, and peered out. He looked around the yard, then stepped back inside and closed it. For a moment, he studied Griffin, his eyes narrowed in suspicion. Then he shrugged and started down the hall, knocking Griffin to one side as he walked past.

Griffin lowered a shoulder and shoved back. Caught by surprise, Sergei stumbled. Arms flailing, he tripped over the bench. He hissed in pain when his injured hand collided with one of the coat hooks. Almost immediately, a crimson stain began spreading across the dressing.

Griffin stared wide-eyed at the blood. Before he could speak, Sergei scrambled to his feet. A thin red line seeped out from under the bandage and trickled down his arm.

"You're dead." Sergei flung out his uninjured hand.

A blast of Wind knocked Griffin off his feet and sent him flying backwards down the hall. His already bruised head whacked against the newel post as he crashed into a heap at the foot of the stairs. Stars popped across his vision. He blinked, trying to clear his head, then rolled over and pushed upright. While he sat rubbing his tender scalp, a shadow fell across him.

Sergei stood over him, his bandaged hand pressed against his tee shirt. "If these sutures have pulled open, I'm coming back and beating the you-know-what out of you. With one hand." He spun on his heels and stormed off to the kitchen.

"Yeah, bring it," Griffin muttered as he grabbed the railing and levered himself up, his head still spinning. He listened for a moment and then yelled. "Well?"

"You lucked out," Sergei hollered back. "Guess I'll save your butt kicking for next time."

Griffin blew out a long breath. *Heck, I could have taken him. I think. Maybe.*

He plodded up the stairs. *This might be a good time to see what Katie's up to. Get out of here for awhile before we kill each other.* He pulled his cell out of his pocket and flipped it open, hitting the speed dial as he headed to his room. "Hi, it's me. What are you doing? Me neither. Hey, can I come over?" He touched his head again and winced. "And I might need an icepack."

Katie's Journal: Sunday, February 6th

I realized something a few days ago. Something that my heart knew before my brain did.

I love Griffin. As *Griffin*.

I mean real love, not just because he's my boyfriend, but because he's also my friend. When he came over on Friday, I realized how much I like just hanging out with him. Watching movies. Listening to music. Playing with Bear.

Talking about nothing.

Talking about everything.

And I feel guilty because I'm glad he's human. And we're going to high school together. Maybe go to college together. Have a future.

Darby Karchut

Am I wrong to want him to stay the way he is now? To be human for the rest of his life?

Is that love?

Griffin's Journal: Tuesday, February 8th

I'm getting sick of mac and cheese. And eating dinner by myself.

Seems like they're gone all the time. Between the storm last weekend and the arctic freeze Colorado has been in these last few days, lots of people need us more than ever.

Need Terrae Angeli, I mean. Don't think anyone really needs *me*.

Except Katie. Fire, I wish I could tell her! I feel like I'm lying to her all over again. Which I am.

I don't know what to do. And I can't ask Basil for advice.

Anyway, he acts like I don't exist. He's too busy working with Ser-jerk. When they are home, they spend all their time talking about their last mission. And getting ready for the next one.

I think Ser-jerk saw me using Fire. But he hasn't said anything.

Maybe I should go ahead and tell Basil. Just get it over with.

Basil's Journal: Wednesday, February 9th

These last five days have been simply horrendous! End on end missions with every available Terrae Angeli out in the field. Sergei is doing the work of two Tiros and holding up well. He's very focused. Very resourceful. Very efficient.

It's like working with a robot.

I heard from Sukalli that Nicopolis has been assigned to the Middle East. Personally, I do not believe the other side of the world is far enough.

Sukalli asked me again when I'm going to tell Griffin the truth.

Never would be my choice.

I do not see how knowing the truth could bring him anything but misery.

Chapter Twenty-Four

"Almost done," Griffin whispered. His breath stirred Katie's hair as he pressed his cheek against her temple. "Just a few more minutes."

"Griffin, it's a dance, not a...a *Proelium*." She smiled, tightening her arms around his neck as they rotated around the dance floor. "Sorry," she called over his shoulder when they bumped into another couple. "That's like our fifth time."

"It's me. I should have practiced more." He peeked out of the corner of his eye at another couple, the girl wincing as she rubbed her bruised foot while her date hovered red-faced nearby. "Of course, I'm not as bad as some."

When the song ended, Griffin groaned with relief and slumped against her. "Whew—made it."

"Oh, get off of me, you goof." She placed her hands on his chest and pushed him away. "Let's go find our jackets before they kick us out of here."

As the band thanked the audience for a mind-bending evening, they made their way to the bleachers piled with coats. After a few minutes of digging, they retrieved their jackets and headed out the double doors with the crowd.

"Hey! It's snowing." Katie stopped and held out her sleeve as the flakes drifted down.

"Wow. Like it hasn't done *that* all winter," Griffin said, his good mood soured. *Guess that means Basil and Ser-jerk are going to be working overtime. And then I get to hear him brag about all his missions.* Annoyance clouded his face as he walked on ahead.

A dull thump and cry of pain yanked him around.

Katie sat crumpled on the sidewalk, her face screwed up while she clutched her ankle. "I-I slipped on some ice," she moaned, blinking back tears while she rocked back and forth.

He rushed over and knelt down. "What hurts?"

She sniffed. "Just my ankle. But my bottom's getting wet," she said, wiping her nose with the back of her glove.

"Here, let me get you up." He slid an arm under her legs and the other around her back. "Hang on to me. As tight as you can." After Katie wrapped her arms around his neck, he shifted his feet under him and scooped her up with a grunt. *This looks so easy in the movies. In real life, not so much.* "You still okay?" he said aloud, hoisting her more securely in his arms while he headed down the sidewalk to the car.

She nodded as she clung to him, wincing as her twisted ankle bounced up and down with each stride. "Ow—not so fast."

"Sorry."

Reaching the Saab, they both sighed with relief. Griffin halted by the passenger side and lowered her down. "Hold on to the roof and keep your weight off your foot." He unlocked the door, guided her inside, and helped her swing her leg around. When Katie bent down to remove her boot, he put out a hand and stopped her. "No, don't. If it's sprained, then we need to keep the boot on for support."

After closing her door, he darted around to the driver's side and hopped in. He revved the engine, then flipped on the heater as Katie began shivering. "Home in five minutes," he murmured and peeled away from the curb in a spray of snow.

* * *

Griffin's Fire

"Would you like to say goodnight?" Lewis leaned over the banister with a wave, then smiled as Griffin hurried up the stairs. "You were right—it's just a mild sprain," he added, slapping him on the back with a wink. "My daughter can be a bit of a drama queen."

"It's a girl thing," Griffin replied without thinking. He blushed and glanced uneasily at Lewis, who just chuckled.

Pausing outside the half-opened door, Lewis rapped softly. "Fair lady? Your knight awaits," he called, then shooed Griffin inside. "Five minutes, young man."

"Yes, sir." Griffin stepped over to the bed, grinning at Katie reclining like a modern-day princess in hoodie and sweatpants, her foot nestled on a thick pillow while an icepack covered her ankle.

"What is it with us and holidays? First Thanksgiving, then Christmas, now Valentine's Day," she said, holding out her arms to him.

"Hey, we made it through Presidents' Day without a major crisis," he joked. He leaned over for a quick kiss, bracing his hands on either side of her. "I have something for you," he whispered in her ear. "I'll bring it over tomorrow."

"I'll be here," she whispered back. She looked down. Her face grew warm at the sight of his tanned hand against her white sheets.

Griffin straightened and glanced over his shoulder. "I better go—your dad's timing me. See you later." He kissed her forehead, then left, closing the door behind him.

Katie listened to his footsteps fading away. She reached over and pressed her fingertips on the spot beside her pillow where his hand had laid a moment before.

It was hot from his touch.

* * *

A few hours later, Griffin shifted in his seat in his open window. Opening the gift box on his lap, he wrinkled his nose at the scent of perfumed tissue paper; he removed the glass rose from its wrappings and held it up by the stem and examined it one last time. The pinks and greens of the crystal glowed in the light of the streetlamp. *I hope she likes it, even though Valentine's Day not until Monday.* He stared across the street. *This is so crazy! Even if I tell her I climbed up her porch and on to her roof, she's going to be suspicious. But I think it will make her happy. To discover it outside her window when she wakes up.*

"Oh, what the heck," he muttered and checked the neighborhood. Cradling the gift in one hand, he turned sideways and slid down the roof in a snowboarder's crouch. His bare feet left dark furrows in the white blanket. Several icicles broke loose with a tinkling sound when he shot past the rain gutter and vanished. A moment later, he landed outside Katie's window. He pushed his windblown hair out of his eyes and peeped in.

For several minutes, Griffin gazed at her sleeping form while snowflakes melted on his face. A realization swept through him like a warm breeze. He cleared his throat.

"Love you," he whispered, his breath misting on the glass. He looked around, embarrassed someone might have heard him. *I've never said that to anyone.* With a smile, he positioned the flower on the window ledge.

Then he turned, took a running start down the sloping roof, and somersaulted off the edge. He disappeared in mid air.

Re-appearing outside his window, he paused to dry his feet on the legs of his sweatpants, then slipped inside. He hopped down and eased the window shut, grimacing as it squealed, and twitched the drapes closed. Humming under his breath, he reached over to the nearby nightstand and snapped on the lamp.

And froze in horror.

Sergei lounged at his desk with one foot propped up on top of Griffin's schoolbooks.

Griffin's Fire

Chapter Twenty-Five

"Well, well," Sergei said. "That's a hell of a secret you've been keeping."

"W-what do you mean?"

"You know what I mean." Tilting back in the chair, Sergei clasped his hands behind his head. "So what does this make you? A born-again angel?"

Bile burned Griffin's throat as panic knotted his guts. "Sergei, please. Please don't tell. Okay?" He licked his lips, trying to swallow. "I'm begging—"

"*That* is a great idea." Sergei dropped his foot and sat up. Beaming, he pointed to the floor in front of him.

Griffin frowned in confusion.

"Begging," Sergei elaborated. "You know. Like on your knees." He waited.

Griffin gritted his teeth. Taking a deep breath, he forced his legs to walk around the bed. For a moment, they glared at each other, then he lowered himself to one knee. "There. Made your day?"

"Actually, my year. Oh, but don't get up just yet," he said when Griffin tried to rise. "I've decided there are two more things I want before I promise to keep your secret identity...well, a secret."

"What are they?"

"First," Sergei said, holding up a finger, "you'll do all my chores around here as well as wait on me. And I get first dibs on the bathroom at all times."

"And the other one?"

Sergei held up a second finger, his eyes gleeful. "Dump Katie. Tomorrow. Without telling her why."

"What?" Griffin jumped to his feet. "No! No way. I know what you're trying to do. But it's not going to work. Believe me—she won't have anything to do with you."

"Sure she will. I'll be incredibly charming. And sympathetic. She won't know what hit her."

"And if I refuse?"

"Then I guess I'll be waiting downstairs tonight for Basil to return. And you and I both know his honor runs too deep for him *not* to inform Command." Sergei settled back. "Which is why you haven't told him, right? Afraid of what he'll do?"

Panic clawed at Griffin. *Oh, God, what do I do? I can't hurt Katie. I can't break her heart just to save myself. But I won't go back to being mortal, either. Go through all that pain again. Lose everything again.*

He looked at Sergei. "How do I know you'll keep your word?" he asked, stalling for time.

"You don't. But you really don't have much of a choice. Sucks, I know." He raised his eyebrows. "So does this mean yes?"

Griffin turned his back on Sergei, trying to summon his courage. Squeezing his eyes tight, he fought the fear tearing at his insides. Fought to make the right decision.

And lost.

Sick with self-loathing, he spun around and tightened his jaw. "Just so you know," he said hoarsely, his brown eyes smoldering as he stared down into Sergei's blue ones. "If you break your promise and tell, then I'm coming after you. And we'll settle it Element to Element."

Sergei stood, his handsome face twisted. "Anytime, anywhere, *brother.*"

Griffin's Fire

They both turned their heads at the sound of the front door opening. Sergei shoved the chair out of the way. "It begins now," he said. "I'll be down shortly for tea. Some strong Russian tea—not that wimpy English kind." He sneered and left, the bathroom door closing behind him with a thump.

Griffin shut his eyes, one hand covering his face. After a moment, he dropped his arm and walked out of his room. Gripping the banister, he negotiated the stairs on unsteady legs. Hearing Basil in his study, he paused in the hallway and scrubbed his face with his tee shirt, then took a deep breath and stuck his head around the corner.

"Hey."

The Mentor turned from his computer, minimizing the screen with a practiced move. "You're up quite late." He looked at Griffin. "And how was the dance?"

"Good. It was…good." He gestured toward the kitchen. "I'm going to make tea. Do you want any?"

Basil lifted an eyebrow. "Did something happen this evening?"

"No. I mean, yes. Katie fell and twisted her ankle on our way home. But it was no big deal. Her dad said she'll be up limping around by tomorrow. That's all."

"Are you sure that's all?"

"Well, yes. Why do you ask?"

"One, because you are a terrible liar. Two, you never, ever drink tea. And three, I know that expression." He stood up and walked around his desk. Laying a hand on Griffin's shoulder, he gave him a shake. "So I will inquire once more. Did something happen? That I can help with?"

Griffin tightened his jaw and stared at the floor. *Yeah, Basil. My whole life is screwed up. I don't have anyone I can trust and I have to hurt a friend to save myself. Please help me. Please tell me what to do.*

"Nah, it's all good." He shrugged off the Mentor's hand and walked away.

Basil stood in the doorway, watching. "A bloody terrible liar."

Darby Karchut

Chapter Twenty-Six

Katie's Journal: Saturday, February 12th
 I can't believe he did that!
 My rose is gorgeous, and it will last forever. (Of course, I'm still going to kick his butt for climbing up on my roof during a snow storm!)
 I showed it to Mom, but didn't tell her where he left it. She said it was a nice alternative to the flower-giving tradition and very romantic. I think him carrying me in his arms was even more romantic. It was so worth spraining my ankle!
 I can't wait to see him today.

* * *

Leaning against the counter, Griffin ran a thumb across the scar on his lip while he gazed out the window at the gray morning and waited for the coffee maker to cease its complaining. He dropped his hand at the sound of footsteps behind him.

"Good morning, lad." Basil walked over and joined him. He peered out at the falling snow. "Classic February day, eh?"

Griffin nodded. He would never admit it, but he was suddenly grateful for Basil standing next to him. Steady and solid as a fortress. He sighed. *Maybe I should go ahead and just tell him. Stop all this sneaking around and lying. Hell, if I get turned again, it won't make my life much different than it is now. And I won't have to hurt Katie.* He swallowed and took a deep breath.

"Basil?"

"Fin."

His courage seeped away.

"Looks like the coffee's ready," he said. Forcing a grin on his face, he filled a cup and hurried out of the kitchen before Basil could say anything. Balancing the mug carefully, he walked upstairs and nudged Sergei's half-open door with his knee before easing inside.

"About time." Sergei swiveled around on his chair and laid his book facedown on the desk. He reached for the cup and took a sip, then grimaced. "It's not warm enough," he complained, handing it back.

Tightening his lips, Griffin cupped it in his palm until steam began rising. After a few moments, he handed the mug over, then turned to leave. He paused in the doorway when Sergei spoke behind him.

"And don't forget our arrangement. I'll be waiting to play my role."

Without looking back, Griffin nodded once and left.

* * *

"Katie—we're leaving. Make sure your cell phone is on." Helen stood in the hallway, rummaging through her purse for the car keys. She glanced up as her daughter, still dressed in sweats and a hoodie, limped down the stairs. "We should be home by late afternoon depending on the weather and traffic in Denver."

"What are you going to do while Dad's giving his seminar?" Katie asked when she reached the bottom step, one arm hugging the newel post.

"Why, spend the day at the Tattered Cover bookstore, of course! Pick up a couple of books on my must-read list. Then maybe do a little shopping for new shoes afterwards. Can't have too many of either." Mother and daughter grinned at each other, and then Helen reached over and tapped her on the nose. "I don't want Griffin over here all day. Two hours max. Understand? And you're not to go over there unless Basil is home."

"Yeah, yeah."

At that moment, Lewis hurried out of the den, juggling his briefcase in one hand while he sorted through the papers inside. "I think I have everything," he said as he snapped it closed. "You ready?" Taking his wife's elbow, he looked at his daughter as they headed out the door. "Be good."

Katie hobbled to the kitchen and waved at her parents as they backed down the driveway. Pulling her cell out of her hoodie's pocket, she placed it on the table and sat down. She winced when she eased her foot up on a chair.

Bear rose from his bed and took a bow before walking over and laying his long head in her lap. Twirling the tuffs of hair sprouting over his eyes into spikes, she laughed, then looked up at the clock. "Any minute now," she said to the dog.

Her phone rang. "Hi, you," she said. "Yeah, I'm in kitchen. No, they just left, but Mom said only for two hours. No, come over now. 'Kay. Bye." Laying her phone down, she pointed toward the kennel in the corner. "And you're taking a nap so we can eat a late breakfast without you trying to crawl into his lap." She grabbed Bear's collar for support and rose, balancing awkwardly. "His lap is already spoken for."

* * *

Griffin thumbed his cell off and slumped back on his bed. *Maybe I could tell her the truth about me and we could keep it a secret just between us. Play Sergei's game until I figure out what to do.* His face brightened with hope for a moment, then faded.

Oh, yeah, that would be cool, asking a friend to lie for me. And then what?

Griffin's Fire

Now both of us will have to sneak around just to see each other? Hardly worth it. But I can't go back to being a mortal. I can't. I won't!

Sure you could, said the Voice. *It's not like you're a full-fledged Terrae Angelus. It's not like you're going on missions or anything. Let's face it. You're not much of an angel and you're not much of a mortal.*

"I'm not much of anything," he whispered, then rolled off the bed and trudged downstairs.

He slipped out the front door and walked slowly across the street, self-disgust weighing his footsteps. Lingering by the angel statue near the Heflin's porch, he started to brush the snow off its head, then stopped himself when he looked into its face. He turned away and climbed the steps.

Katie opened the door before he could ring the bell, hanging on the knob for balance as she flung an arm around his neck. "I love it—I love my rose! That was so sweet of you." She pulled back and slapped his arm. "But I could kill you for climbing up there. You could have just brought it over this morning."

"Katie, we need to talk about—"

"I showed it to Mom," she continued as she ushered him inside and shut the door. "But I didn't tell her you left it outside on my windowsill. She would have freaked!"

"No doubt. Listen, Katie. There's something—"

"Do you want some breakfast? I haven't eaten yet, either."

"Katie!" He winced at the sound of his own harsh voice. "Katie," he tried again, "I have to talk to you about something." He took her arm and helped her into the living room, guiding her over to the sofa.

"What's going on?" She sank down, a line appearing between her brows. "You're all serious this morning. Did something happen?"

Chewing on the inside of his cheek, he paced back and forth in front of her a few turns, then walked over to the bay window and stared out, forcing himself to begin. "Since you met me, have you ever thought about maybe dating other guys?"

Darby Karchut

"What other guys?"

"You know. *Normal* guys. Guys who know what to do at dances and stuff."

"What? And miss all the fun of training you?" she joked.

"That's what I mean. Maybe you should date someone else who already knows what to do."

Her smile faded. "Why would I do that?"

Griffin spoke over his shoulder. "Because it might be good for you. To go out with someone who doesn't have the whole I-used-to-be-an-angel baggage."

"Okay, where did this all come from? Was it the dance? Or because I fell?"

"No! No, it wasn't you or anything you did. Never think that. Okay?" He braced his hands on the windowsill and dropped his head. "This is about me. And how screwed up I am. Which isn't fair to you."

"Are you telling me...wait...are you...are you breaking up with me?"

He closed his eyes at the tremor in Katie's voice. Clearing his throat, he struggled to keep his voice normal. "You know, Sergei told me I was crazy to quit seeing you. He thinks you're amazing and that I'm insane to let you go."

"Why are you saying all this?" She stood up, holding on to the arm of the sofa. "And why are you talking with *Sergei* about *us?*" Katie limped over. Grabbing his arm, she pulled him around. "Griffin, this is not like you. You're not making any sense."

He stepped away, his heart in shreds. "I know. And I know I'm hurting you right now. But in the end, you'll be better off without me." His throat tightened when the first tear rolled down her face; his eyes burned. "I'm sorry," he choked. He brushed past her and fled.

Yanking the door open, he bolted outside. Unable to see, he paused for a moment blinking up at the sky, then jumped off the porch and broke into a run. He sprinted down the street toward the park, his feet churning up puffs of snow. Wheeling into the empty playground, he slowed down, then stopped, his chest heaving as he stared at the tire swing. He dragged his sleeve roughly across his face as he walked over and wrapped an arm around the support post. Pressing his forehead against the frosty metal, he squeezed his eyes shut at the memory of their first kiss. After a long minute, he straightened up.

With a cry, he smashed his fist into the iron pole.

* * *

Sergei peered out his window, smiling while he watched Griffin race away. "Show time," he said. He smoothed his blue sweater, then walked down the stairs and out the front door. Whistling under his breath, he followed Griffin's footprints through the snow toward Katie's house.

Chapter Twenty-Seven

Basil's Journal: Sunday, February 13th
    Yesterday, without any warning, Griffin broke off his relationship with Katie. (Helen informed me last night when they returned from Denver to a teary daughter.)
    They have parted ways after being inseparable for almost half a year. Katie is devastated and Helen and Lewis are heartbroken. For both teens.
    I tried repeatedly all day to discover the reason behind it, but he's back to his old pattern of keeping everything locked away.

Katie's Journal: Thursday, February 17th
    I don't know if I miss him more or hate him more.
    Every time I see him across the street or at school, I get so upset I want to cry.
    And then I do.
    He looks as miserable as I feel! So why did he do it?
    Sergei came by again this afternoon. He said he wanted to see how I was doing. He only stayed a few minutes (must be getting the message) but he gave me his cell number in case I need someone to talk to.
    No way! I want *my* angel back! So I can punch him out.
    And then kiss him.

* * *

Griffin squatted down and ran his fingers back and forth over the spines of the books packed on the lowest shelf. He stopped and checked the list in his hand, then searched again. Locating the correct volume, he stood and began flipping through it. A soft intake of breath broke the silence of the library. He glanced up.

Katie stood at the end of the aisle. For a long minute, they looked at each other.

Pressing her lips into a thin line, she edged forward between the tall stacks. She raised her chin and gestured toward the shelf behind him. "If you don't mind, I need to get a book from that section."

"Oh, right." Griffin shuffled to one side. "Sorry," he added when she moved past him.

She hesitated for a moment. "For being in my way or for being a jerk?"

"Well, both, I guess."

"Too late, don't you think?"

Griffin's face burned. Without a word, he spun on his heels and walked away. Behind him, Katie blinked back tears as she stared at his retreating back.

* * *

"Friday afternoon and *I* get stuck helping Zimmerman scrap clay off the tables," Griffin grumbled under his breath. He slammed his locker door shut; the staccato rattle of metal echoed through the deserted hallway. Slinging his book bag over a shoulder, he headed toward the exit door, then stopped.

He frowned in confusion at the sound of angry voices around the corner. A familiar one rose in frustration. Griffin broke into a run and raced toward the next hall.

When he shot around the corner, he spotted an older boy shoving Cas Navarre against the wall next to an open locker. At the same time, a second boy ransacked Cas' backpack.

A red haze flooded Griffin's vision. All the fury and heartache of the last few days broke over him like a wave. He flung his bag to one side and sped up.

"Cas!"

Sprinting full out, Griffin lowered a shoulder and plowed into the boy with the pack, knocking him off his feet. The boy flew through the air and landed on his back, then slid across the floor. His head smacked into the baseboard with a resounding *thunk*.

In a blur of motion, Griffin spun on his heels and flung up an arm. Blocking the second boy's punch with ease, he shoved him backwards into the open locker. Wedged tightly, the boy kicked his legs, his arms and shoulders pinned in the narrow opening.

Before he could wiggle free, Griffin stepped closer and slapped both of his hands on either side of the locker's frame; the metal began glowing. He grinned at the first yelp of pain.

"Stop!" The boy shrieked, thrashing about in desperation. "You're burning my arms!"

Griffin let go. The surface cooled rapidly. "Shove Cas around again and it'll be your face next time." He grabbed the front of the boy's shirt and yanked him free. Matching stripes of charred fabric branded the boy's sleeves. "Take your buddy and get out of here." He watched as the two boys staggered away.

"Thanks," Cas said, stooping to collect his pack. He stuffed crumbled papers and books back inside and zipped it closed with an irritated yank. "Man, that's the second time this week those guys tried that."

"What were they doing?"

"Shake down."

"Shake down?"

"You know. Stealing. Robbing me." He picked up his bag and hoisted it over his shoulder. "Dude, what century are you from?"

Well, technically, this one, Griffin thought. *Since I was created only six years ago.* "Are you going to tell your dad?" he asked as they headed toward the front office. He paused to snatch up his own pack.

"Heck, no! And don't you either! It's bad enough he works here. I don't want people thinking I go crying to him with problems."

"All right—I get it. But listen, Cas. If those guys try anything like that again, will you at least tell *me*? And I'll back you up."

Cas chuckled. "What are you, my guardian angel or something?"

Griffin missed a step and stumbled. "What? No. I'm just...you know...your friend." They turned down the main corridor. The warmth of the late afternoon sun poured through the wall of glass.

"So." Cas cleared his throat. "How did you do that?"

"How did I do what?"

"Burn that guy's arms."

Griffin shrugged. "They weren't burned. He just got them pinched in the locker." He held his breath, waiting to see if his friend believed him.

Cas looked at him. He opened his mouth, and then closed it again. "Listen, you want a ride home?" he asked instead, gesturing toward the school's reception area. "Dad's usually done by four thirty. We could hang out in his office. Do some homework."

Griffin shook his head with a private sigh of relief. "Nah, thanks anyway. I'll catch you later." He peeled off toward the main door and pushed it open. Before he could step outside, Cas spoke behind him.

"Hey, Griffin?"

He paused and looked back. "Yeah?"

Cas glanced around the empty hall, then stepped closer. "Why *did* you and Katie break up?"

"Because I'm an idiot, Cas." *And a coward.*

Twenty minutes later, he arrived home. Nudging the front door shut with his heel, Griffin dropped his book bag on the bench and shrugged out of his jacket. He made a face when a voice spoke from the living room.

Darby Karchut

"It's about time," Sergei called. "Basil wants the dishes done. And make me a snack before you get started."

Griffin stepped into the archway and glared at Sergei stretched out on the sofa flipping through one channel after another. "Where is he?"

"Where do you think? Said he'll be home in time for dinner." Sergei sat up and propped his feet on the coffee table. "Well? What part of 'get me a snack' didn't you understand?"

Swallowing a retort that would have shocked Basil, he stalked past Sergei toward the kitchen. After pulling a bag of trail mix from the cupboard, he grabbed a soft drink from the refrigerator. Heading back, he tossed both items in Sergei's lap on his way toward the hall. He mentally kicked himself for not giving the soda can a good shake.

"I went over and saw Katie again a few days ago," Sergei said, popping the can open with a snap and a hiss.

Griffin froze in the doorway. "So?"

Sergei took a drink before speaking. "So she's being coy—I can hardly get her to talk to me. But I rather like that whole ice maiden routine of hers. It'll make it more rewarding when she finally agrees to go out with me."

Griffin turned around. "Oh, Katie isn't being coy. She just has good taste."

"Then why did she ever date you?" With a smirk, Sergei pointed his finger at Griffin and sent a blast of Wind into his face.

Stumbling back a step, Griffin winced, his eyes stinging. "You butt," he said under his breath and stomped his foot. A shock wave traveled across the room. Just as Sergei took another sip, the sofa bucked. Soda spilled down his chin.

"Sorry," Griffin said. "My foot slipped."

Slamming his drink down, Sergei jumped up and flung out both hands. Griffin crashed against the far wall of the hall, the impact knocking the air out of him. Before he could recover, Sergei materialized in front of him. He grabbed him by the shoulders and pinned him in place.

"Do you really want to take *me* on?" Sergei said softly, their face inches apart. His fingers dug into Griffin's arms.

Griffin stared back. "I was just about to ask you the same question."

"Oh, real funny. Let's see who's laughing when I tell Basil about your new flight status."

"Right. Like you would. Hell, you have as much to lose as I do. If you admit you blackmailed me, you lose your own personal slave *and* a chance at dating Katie. So go ahead—tell him. If you got the juice." He sneered. "Which I doubt." He tensed as Sergei snarled and drew back his fist.

The blow never fell.

A thud outside the house, followed by another, froze them in place. They both stared wide-eyed at the front door, listening to the sound of Basil stomping the snow off his boots on the porch.

Without a word, Sergei let go and pushed Griffin toward the archway. "Look busy," he hissed, then shot up the stairs. Griffin tugged his shirt in place as he ran across the living room and into the kitchen. He yanked the dishwasher open and grabbed an armload of dirty dishes from the sink and began dumping them in the machine. Forks and spoons tumbled pell-mell with a clinking sound into the tray. He kneed the door shut as Basil walked in.

"Why hello, lad," Basil said, heading straight for the sink. "Good day?" he asked, flipping on the water. He scrubbed his hands, muck and grease swirling down the drain.

Griffin stepped to one side. "Yeah. I guess." *Apart from Sergei almost going World War Three on me.* "Except these guys were hassling Cas after school, so I—"

"Is Sergei home?" Basil said, drying his hands.

"In his room. Why?"

Basil ignored the question. Tilting his face toward the ceiling, he raised his voice. "Sergei, come downstairs." Footsteps thudded overhead as he tossed the towel back on the counter. "I'm sorry, what were you going to tell me? About Cas?"

As Griffin opened his mouth, Sergei dashed into the kitchen. "What's up, Basil?"

The Mentor turned. "We're needed at the airport as soon as you can be ready."

"I'm ready now," Sergei said, already thrusting his arms into his jacket. "Let's roll."

"Right." With a nod, Basil led the way out the back. "I'm not certain when we'll be home, Fin. Mind you don't stay up too late."

Nighty night, mouthed Sergei, sneering over his shoulder as he followed. The door closed behind them. It rattled from the blast of their departure.

Griffin stood in the middle of the empty room. The stillness of the house pressed around him.

Griffin's Fire

Chapter Twenty-Eight

Basil's Journal: Thursday, February 24th
Another dreadful week in our home. There is so much tension around here the weight of it is forming a black hole.

Frankly, even I am beginning to see that this situation is not feasible. I cannot train Sergei and raise Griffin in the same household. It's like trying to mix...

Like trying to mix Fire and Water.

But Heaven help Command if they force me to send Fin away. Because then they will have lost *two* Terrae Angeli.

After all, a promise is a promise.

Griffin, poor lad, isn't sleeping well; he picks at his food and his schoolwork is slipping even more. He's also very moody and spends most of his time in his room.

Lena suspects something.

* * *

"And just what are you doing awake at this untimely hour?"

Griffin jumped at the sudden voice. Pausing in the middle of the kitchen, he looked over at the back door.

Basil stood there, muddy boots in one hand, his clothing soaked with melting snow, and dripping water on the tile floor. With a frown, he dumped his shoes on a mat in the corner and glanced at the clock. "You do realize it is five forty-five in the morning," he said, pointing his fingers at his wet clothes. Puffs of air flattened his sweater against his chest as he dried himself.

"I've got to finish something." Griffin dropped his math book on the table before heading to the overworked coffee machine already laboring away on the counter. *Anyway*, he thought, *why do you care what time I get up?*

Face averted to hide a scowl, Griffin filled his cup, added some milk, then sat down and opened his text. Pulling out a worksheet, he hunched over it, twiddling his pencil in one hand.

Basil walked over and joined him. "Algebra, eh?"

"Yeah."

"May I help you?"

You can leave me alone. Griffin shook his head as he shifted in his chair, his eyes fixed on the page. "I need to figure it out myself so I know the steps," he added aloud when Basil rose and poured himself a cup.

"Would you care for something to eat? Perhaps an omelet?"

"No, thanks." His lips pressed into a thin line as he erased an answer for the second time.

"Well, you need more than coffee for breakfast." Basil opened the refrigerator and began rummaging about.

"Nah, I'm good." Griffin twisted around, his back to the Mentor while he tried to concentrate. *Why the heck doesn't this equation balance?*

Basil hooked an arm over the open fridge door. "How about juice and a bagel?"

"How about you shut up and let me concentrate," Griffin said under his breath.

An ominous silence filled the kitchen for a moment.

Griffin flinched when an iron hand clamped down on the back of his neck and squeezed. Hard.

"And how about you curb your tongue."

"Basil, I'm trying to get this done." Griffin snarled in frustration. "You're always hassling me about school. Then when I'm working on it, you keep bugging me." He jumped up and shrugged off Basil's hand. "Anyway, don't you have another mission with your pet Tiro or something?" Snatching up his materials, he stormed out of the kitchen.

Basil stood frozen, listening to Griffin as he stomped upstairs. He looked down at the empty table, lost in thought. Then he headed over to the cupboard and pulled out a cardboard box.

An hour later, Griffin tiptoed back down the stairs. He eased his book bag from around the newel post, then snuck out the front door.

He paused to check across the street. All clear. Running down the steps and across the lawn, he kept his eyes fixed on the sidewalk as he jogged past Katie's house through the falling snow, not looking up until he turned the corner.

Griffin slowed to a walk. Cupping his hand, he ignited a ball of flames and threw it at a frozen puddle. With a hiss, the ice melted into slush. *I really shouldn't be doing this stuff in public*, he thought, and then pointed a finger. A stream of fire erupted from its tip. In large letters, he wrote his name across an unmarred stretch of snow-covered lawn. *Don't think I really care.*

Reaching the high school, Griffin crossed the courtyard and headed toward the media center. He paused at the door to stomp the snow off his shoes and nod at the librarian.

"Hi, Mrs. Guthrie," he said, trying not to stare at her tattoo crawling out of her shirt collar and creeping up her neck. He wove his way around already occupied tables to a secluded corner. Dropping his bag beside him, he sat down. His stomach rumbled. *I wish I had taken Basil's offer for breakfast.* The harsh words he had thrown at the Mentor kept playing over and over in his head.

Griffin made a face. He flung his bag up on the table and opened it, searching for his unfinished homework.

Several granola bars tumbled out.

"Oh." Griffin picked up the nearest one and smoothed the wrapper, the plastic crinkling under his fingers. *Oh, nice move, Ba-*

Darby Karchut

sil. Way to make me feel even worse for being a jerk. With a wry grin, he peeled it open and took a bite. He shoved the rest of them back into his bag, then started on his homework; his heart lighter.

Half an hour later, Griffin headed out of the library and toward his usual spot around the corner from Katie's locker. Hidden behind a concrete pillar, he gazed at her standing just a few yards away, her head bowed while she sorted through binders and books. *Well, she once joked that guardian angels were like stalkers. Guess she was right.* He found himself smiling as he watched her laughing with a girl at the next locker.

Griffin jumped when the bell rang directly over his head. He whirled around.

And barreled straight into Milton.

They bounced off each other, both staggering backwards. As Griffin watched in horror, Milton fell with a thud. For a moment, he lay stunned on the floor like a shaggy walrus. Graded papers were strewn across the hallway.

"Raine!" Milton roared, his face crimson with rage. He sat up and rubbed his elbow. "You idiot!" He lurched to his feet as another teacher pushed through the gathering crowd. "Vince, would you get the vice principal?" As the other teacher hurried away, Milton narrowed his eyes. "Don't *you* even twitch."

"Mr. Milton, I swear it was an accident. I didn't see you." Griffin tried to ignore the other students clustered nearby, whispering and nudging each other.

"Shut up." Milton flexed his arm a few times and looked around. "And the rest of you—get to class." He continued to glare at Griffin while the hall emptied.

"Mr. Milton, I really didn't—"

"I said, SHUT UP!" Spittle sprayed from his mouth. He started toward Griffin, then stopped at the sound of running footsteps. They both turned to look.

The vice principal shot around the corner, his Loony Tunes tie fluttering over one shoulder. "What happened here?" he panted.

"Sir, I ran into —"

"This student assaulted me," Milton said, massaging his arm again as he screwed up his face in pain. "Knocked me down. Vince saw everything."

"No, I didn't. I just ran into him. By accident."

"You sure it was intentional, Milt?"

"Yeah, I am." Milton twisted his mouth. "Why? You think I'm lying?"

The vice principal sighed. "What's your name, son?" he asked, pulling a cell phone out of his pocket. Milton hid a smile as he bent over and began collecting the scattered papers.

"Griffin Raine. But I didn't do it on purpose. I just didn't want to be late for—"

The vice principal held up a finger as he spoke into the phone. "Louise? Check the records for Griffin Raine. See if there's been any disciplinary problems?" He waited a few minutes, then nodded. "Sophomore? Okay, thanks." He thrust the phone back into his pocket and looked at Griffin. "Come with me."

They walked in silence to the office. When they entered the reception area, he swallowed and tried again. "Sir, please believe me. It really was an accident."

The vice principal gestured toward a chair in the corner. "Take a seat. And don't move." He walked around the counter and stuck his head into Navarre's office. "James? Got one of yours out here. Supposedly knocked Milton down in the hallway just now. Do you want to talk with him while I call the parents?"

Griffin leaned forward and buried his head in his hands. Ringing phones and busy voices masked the sound of the approaching figure; he jumped when someone tapped his arm. He looked up into Mr. Navarre's friendly face.

"Let's talk," the counselor said, motioning with his head toward his office.

Griffin followed him. He sank down on a chair by the cluttered desk as Navarre took a seat behind it.

Darby Karchut

"Before we discuss what just happened, Griffin, is there anything else going on? Anything I can help with?"

"Nothing's going on." His eyes flickered once at the photo on Navarre's desk.

"Any problems here at school? Or at home?"

"Nope—it's all good."

Navarre snorted. "Nice try." He looked up when the secretary appeared in the doorway.

"I couldn't reach Mr. Raine," she said. "So I called the other legal guardian listed in his file. She'll be here within the hour."

Griffin slumped lower in his seat as he groaned inside. *And my day just gets better and better.*

* * *

"Hello. I'm Lena Weiss. The school called me about Griffin Raine being suspended?" She hooked her umbrella over her arm while she waited by the counter, then turned around when a voice spoke behind her.

"Ms. Weiss? I'm James Navarre." He shook her hand. "Sophomore counselor. Please follow me." He led the way to his office.

Griffin looked up when they walked in, his eyes wide. "Miss Lena, I didn't—"

"Hush. We'll talk later." She patted his hand as she took a seat next to him. "So, Mr. Navarre. What happens now?"

The counselor leaned a hip on his desk. "The school has a zero tolerance policy for any form of assault. And since he has a history of detentions, unfortunately, this is the next step." Navarre reached behind him and picked up a clipboard. "Griffin has a one day suspension. He'll be expected to make up all assignments when he returns on Monday." He handed the form and a pen to her. "Please sign at the bottom. We tried repeatedly to contact Mr. Raine, but couldn't reach him."

"No doubt. But you were right to call me," she said while she wrote, then handed the paper back. "May I take him home now?"

"Yes, but before you leave…" He paused and looked over at Griffin. "Like we discussed earlier, Mr. Milton may have overreacted. But we have to jump through these hoops, okay?" He waited until Griffin nodded, and then continued. "And remember, you're still welcome at our house anytime." He stood up with a smile. "I'll tell you the same thing I tell Cas. You are the sum of your choices in life, son. One bad choice doesn't make you a bad person."

Griffin nodded again. *I wish I believed that.* He stood up and waited as Miss Lena and Navarre spoke for a few more minutes, then they headed outside into the growing storm.

"Are you mad at me?" Griffin asked while they walked toward Lena's car, the wind tugging at the umbrella he held over her gray curls. He noticed her gray hair was almost white; he kept one hand on her elbow.

"Angry? No. Worried? Very much."

After helping her into her seat, Griffin trotted around to the other side, tossing the umbrella into the back. As he settled into the passenger side, he glanced over. "So now what?"

"You're coming home with me until Basil is available. I left him a message about the suspension. I could use some help organizing my library and you just volunteered, yes?"

"Yes, ma'am."

They drove north on the interstate, the wiper blades slapping at the falling snow. Griffin stared out of the window. *Basil's going to kill me. Or lock me in my room until summer. No. Wait. He'll kill me,* then *lock my body in my room until summer.*

He rubbed his temple. *Nice of Mr. Navarre to tell me all that, though. Cas is the only friend I've got left. I wonder what he's going to think when he hears about this?*

Darby Karchut

Twenty-five minutes later, they pulled into the garage. Griffin winced when he banged his door against a large packing crate. "Looks like you're moving."

"I am. This house is too large for me anymore." She threaded through stacks of boxes as she led the way into the kitchen. After folding her coat over a chair, she pushed up her sleeves. "Strudel and juice. And a talk." She pointed to the kitchen table. "Sit."

"Need any help?" he asked, dumping his bag on the floor beside him.

"No, it will just take me a minute." She bustled about the kitchen, shortly placing a thick wedge of pastry in front of him. The scent of baked apples and cinnamon warmed the room. As Griffin dug in, Lena joined him at the table. She peered over the top of her glasses, her eyes thoughtful.

"Basil is worried about you, *liebling*."

"I know," he said, his mouth full.

"He's mentioned some changes in your behavior that have us both concerned."

He swallowed. "What do you mean?"

Lena reached across the table and placed her fragile hand over one of his. "Are you…are you using drugs?"

Griffin's mouth fell open as his fork hit the plate with a clatter. "Drugs?" he said in disbelief. "You and Basil think I'm doing *drugs*?" He grinned and shook his head, his eyes dancing. "Yeah, that's it, Miss Lena. I'm hooked on…wait for it…*angel* dust."

Lena smacked his arm. "I am quite serious about this."

"I'm sorry, but come on—I've only been mortal for like eight weeks. I wouldn't even know who to get the stuff from, much less how to use it." He took her hand and squeezed it. "And I may be one messed up ex-angel who's done some pretty stupid things, but I'm not *that* stupid," he said, looking her straight in the eye.

She stared at him for a few moments, and then let out a sigh of relief. "*Mein Gott*. What I have been imagining…" she muttered, then stopped when she heard the Saab roar into the driveway, its tires squealing as it skidded to a halt.

"Oh, dear," Lena said.

"Oh, crap," muttered Griffin.

Chapter Twenty-Nine

Miniature porcelain angels clinked on the glass shelves of Lena's curio cabinet as Basil stomped back and forth across the living room. At each turn, he glared at Griffin slouched on the sofa.

"Suspended."

"Yes, sir."

"Until Monday?"

"Yes, sir."

"For striking a teacher?"

"What? No! I mean, no, sir." Griffin scowled. "It was an *accident*. I ran into him and he fell down. I was hurrying because I was going to be late and I didn't want another detention."

Basil stopped pacing and planted himself in the middle of the room, his hands on his hips. "What in the name of all that is holy has gotten into you lately?"

"Nothing's gotten into me. Unless you count the pile of mortality shoved up my..." He left the sentence unfinished as his eyes flicked briefly toward Lena sitting nearby. Glowering, he crossed his arms over his chest and stared straight ahead. "I don't know what you mean."

"Then let me enlighten you. You deeply wounded Katie by your boorish behavior, you're not taking school seriously, and you're unpleasant to me and to Sergei. When you're not sulking in your room. You hardly eat or sleep. And now you're suspended." He massaged his neck. "Just bloody marvelous."

"Now both of you calm down and we'll..." began Lena. Before she could finish, Griffin jumped to his feet.

"I *am* taking school seriously," Griffin yelled, flinging his arms wide. "I got up at the butt crack of dawn to work on my math, didn't I?" He glanced away, his lips pressed tight. "And anyway, this has nothing to do with Katie. She's happier without me." He looked back at Basil and narrowed his eyes. "And you might not have noticed, since you've been so busy with your new Tiro and all, but I've had a lot dumped on me lately. So sorry I'm not perfect enough for you."

Basil's face darkened as he grabbed Griffin by the shoulders and gave him a shake. "Stop using what happened as an excuse for your recent conduct. I expect the same behavior out of you whether you're mortal or angel."

"Yeah. Well, get used to disappointment. I had to!" Chest heaving, Griffin twisted free and bolted down the hall, ignoring Basil's order to stop. He wrenched the door open and sprinted down the walkway. He vanished into the storm after a few steps.

A gust of wind slapped the limbs of the spruce tree when Griffin materialized in their backyard a few minutes later. Panting, he stood for a moment, hands clasped on top of his head, trying to catch his breath. *Fire, I think that was the longest flight I've made in a month.*

He hurried across the yard, slipped inside, and eased the door closed with a soft snick. The house creaked around him as he listened for any sounds; after a few minutes, he relaxed. Peeling off his shoes and socks, he picked them up and headed upstairs. He checked Sergei's empty bedroom, then continued down the hall to his. Once inside, he pulled off his jacket and tossed it on the chair, then flung himself on his bed, laying spread eagled as he stared at the ceiling.

Basil's going to wonder how I got all the way home from the north end of the city. Maybe I'll just tell him I hitched a ride. Griffin thought for a mo-

Darby Karchut

ment, then made a face. *Yeah, right. Like he'd be okay with that. Never mind. Not such a good idea.*

He rolled over onto his side, stuffing his pillow under his head and rubbing his bare feet together. *I still wonder why? Why I changed back? Why I'm a Terrae Angelus again?* "Am I supposed to learn a lesson?" he said, gazing out the window at the falling snow. "Because I don't think I read that chapter." He closed his eyes. *Or maybe, just maybe, it's something else.*

* * *

The slam of the front door jerked Griffin awake. As he raised his head to listen, a thud, then a second one, followed by a string of Russian words, echoed through the house. Rolling off his bed, he landed soundlessly and tiptoed over to his door. He took a position behind it. Peeking through the crack, he watched as Sergei stumbled up the stairs, his white sweater bloodstained and his proud face twisted in anguish. Griffin lost sight of him when he stepped into his room.

Good thing my door to the bathroom was shut, he thought. He crept over and pressed his ear against it, listening to the whoosh of running water and the sound of a muffled sob. *Yup. Failed mission—I know the sounds. Even if he is a jerk, I better see if he needs any help.*

Straightening up, Griffin knocked on the door. "Hey. You okay?" He frowned when the water abruptly shut off, followed by a drawer banging shut.

"Yeah."

"Need any help?"

"Not from you."

Griffin rolled his eyes. *Of course not.* He walked out and started toward the stairs, glancing at Sergei's closed door as he went by, then headed down to the kitchen.

Griffin's Fire

Scrounging through the pantry for several minutes, he finally decided on crackers and a can of soup. He turned around at the sound of approaching footsteps.

"What are you doing home?" Sergei asked, wearing a fresh shirt; his face scrubbed clean. He sauntered over to the refrigerator and opened it. "Let me guess—they sent you home for running with scissors?"

"None of your business."

Sergei snorted, and then dug in his pocket when his cell phone rang. He thumbed it on as he reached for a soda. "Hello? Yeah, I'm back." He froze, a can in one hand. "Are you serious?" He listened for a few more minutes, then looked over the door at Griffin and grinned. "Actually, Basil, he's right here. Making lunch." Sergei shrugged. "I don't know—maybe the bus? Or he hitchhiked?" he said, then nodded. "Yes. Yes, I'll keep an eye on him. See you soon." He closed the fridge, leaning against it as he tucked his phone away and popped the can. "Someone's in trouble," he said in a sing-song voice. "Basil's on his way home. And he is so far beyond pissed, we're talking about another time zone."

Griffin groaned, all thoughts of food vanishing. He looked over when Sergei chuckled.

"I have got to hand it to you. You can screw up like nobody's business. Is there anything you've done *right* in your life?" He shook his head and slurped his drink.

"Shut up, jerk."

"First you go and tell a human girl you're an angel. And then you *date* her. Really, dude? Next, you fail your *Proelium*, so Command makes you mortal. Then, by some miracle, you get upgraded to angel status, but you blow that second chance." Sergei pulled out a chair and spun it around, straddling it as he rolled the can between his hands. Frost began coating the outside of it with a crackle. "What I can't understand is why Katie is still so in love in with you. And why Basil even bothers."

Griffin's heart leaped at Sergei's words. *Katie loves me?* he almost blurted out. He tucked the thought away, a warm flame in the center of his chest. "Because Basil made a promise," he said instead. "Unlike *your* Mentor. Who hasn't even called you *once* since he dumped you and ran. Of course, I can see why."

Hurt and rage darkened Sergei's face. He rose slowly and knocked the chair out of his way. "Remember that butt kicking I promised you? I think *now* is the perfect time."

"Oh, yeah? Well, you're in the back of a very long line." Griffin squared his shoulders and curled his hands into fists. "But hey! I'd be happy to move you to the front."

They lunged for each other at the same time.

Chapter Thirty

Basil glanced over as the speed limit sign flashed past him. He shrugged. *Merely a suggestion*, he decided as he raced along the highway. Slush sprayed from the Saab's tires like wings.

"Bloody hell!" He stomped the brakes to avoid the slow moving vehicle in front of him. *If I didn't need the bloody car*, he fumed, glaring at the taillights inching along ahead of him through the worsening storm, *I would have been to the bloody house by now. How mortals can stand this day after day is beyond me.* He shifted down and crept along, his fingers drumming on the steering wheel. *I should have told Sergei he had permission to duct tape the lad to a chair until I returned.* He frowned as his thoughts circled back to a seemingly insignificant question.

Just how did Griffin get home so quickly?

* * *

Sergei grabbed the front of Griffin's shirt and flung him sideways into the counter. Griffin winced when his hip struck the edge. Throwing up an arm, he blocked Sergei's incoming fist, then lowered his head and plowed into the other Tiro. Pumping his legs, he propelled Sergei backwards into the refrigerator with a rattling crash.

Griffin's jaw exploded with pain when Sergei brought his knee up sharply and clipped him under the chin. He staggered backwards. Blood from his bitten tongue filled his mouth while stars filled his vision. He shook his head, trying to focus.

"I'm going to freaking kill you!" Sergei started for him

Griffin spat blood. He bared his teeth at Sergei with a red-streaked grimace and made a *come along* motion with his hand. "So you keep saying." His eyes widened when Sergei abruptly vanished. *Oh, this is not good.*

A moment later, a two-ton truck hit Griffin in the chest, sending him flying across the kitchen. He slammed into the back door. It crashed open, all but one hinge ripping loose. One of the window panes shattered and sent glass shards across the patio.

Locked in combat, they wrestled in mid-air before hitting the ground. Tumbling apart, they both skidded across the yard, leaving parallel furrows in the snow. The wind screamed overhead as it rocked the row of evergreens back and forth.

Griffin rolled to his feet. He dove to one side as a jet of Water blasted by his head, ripping apart a leafless bush behind him. Crouching low, he ignited a fireball in each hand, then launched one after the other. He cursed under his breath when Sergei twisted and spun out of the way of Griffin's Fire. It burst against the hedge of trees, singeing the lower branches before winking out.

With a snarl, Sergei flung out his hand. Wind slapped Griffin off his feet and hurled him into the back wall; his skull smacked against the stone. Sprawled on the ground, he blinked as black spots swirled in front of his eyes. *Man, I'm going to have a serious concussion after this. If I survive, that is.* Struggling to his knees, he shook his head clear, then cocked his arm back and drove his fist into the ground with a grunt.

Earth and snow rippled toward Sergei in a wave. He reeled, wind milling his arms, and fell on his hands and knees. With a cry, he threw himself flat when a third fireball whizzed over his head. He scrambled to his feet and sent another torrent of Water at Griffin.

Still on his knees, Griffin pointed his arm. Flames shot from his fingertips. Gasping for breath, he staggered to his feet, his elbow locked as he sent a stream of Fire straight into Sergei's flood. *Wait, wasn't I just here*, he thought. *In December with Nicopolis? What is with these Wind and Water angels?*

"Come on," he growled. "Give it up already." His hair glowed in shades of auburn and espresso in the light of the flames.

Squinting through the blood running into his eyes from a gash on his forehead, Sergei spread his fingers wider. Planting his feet more firmly, he bared his teeth. "No, you first," he gasped. "I insist."

Their eyes met. Then Sergei waved his other hand and let loose another blast of Wind. In desperation, Griffin kicked the toe of his shoe into the ground in front of him. An embankment of dirt sprang up like a shield.

Earth and Wind collided. Muck whirled around them and blinded them. Overhead, the storm's fury increased, adding flying snow to the battlefield.

After a few minutes, the strain of using both of his Elements at the same time began to drag at Griffin. As if leaden weights were attached to his arms and legs. Even his eyelids. *I'm not going to last much longer.* He grimaced as a cramp seized his arm.

Then out of the corner of his eye, he caught a movement by the back door.

* * *

Basil pulled into the driveway and climbed out. "Next time, I'm flying," he muttered, trotting up the porch steps and through the front door. "Griffin!" He stopped himself in time from slamming the door behind him. "You best have a bloody good excuse..." he began; his voice trailed off when he heard the wind whistling through the house. He hurried through the living room toward the kitchen, then broke into a sprint at the sounds of battle and the sight of the door swinging from a single hinge. He leaped through its splintered frame and skidded to a stop. "By the Light," he whispered.

* * *

As Griffin watched, a figure emerged from the house, half hidden by the snowstorm. *Oh, no—not Basil!* He hesitated for a moment, then dropped his hand and leaped into the air.

Sergei gave a shout of victory when Griffin vanished.

Chapter Thirty-One

Helen scribbled another item on her list, then slipped it inside her purse. "Does she want to come with us?" she asked as she rose from the table and picked up her coat from the back of the chair.

"No, I'm afraid not," Lewis said, walking into the kitchen. "She said grocery shopping with her parents ranks quite high in the nerd category or some such adolescent retort." He pulled a fleece cap over his bald head. "Are you ready for your personal chauffeur to take you to the store?"

Helen smiled. "You're sweet to drive me after teaching all day. I feel safer in the SUV with this weather." As they headed out of the kitchen and across the hall, she turned and called up the stairs. "Katie? Don't forget to clean Bear's paws before you let him back in. I just mopped the floor." They exchanged glances at the morose response.

Opening the front door, Helen added, "I could wring his neck for hurting her." She took Lewis's arm as they negotiated the steps. "Except..."

Lewis patted her hand. "Except you miss him, too."

※ ※ ※

Bear pawed at the tool shed door, each stroke of his massive foot rattling the latch. Sniffing at the threshold, he whined, then clawed the door again. He paused and shook his fur clear of snow, his dog tags jangling, then took up his post, his nose pressed against the crack.

"Hey, stupid." Katie hovered in the back doorway, her arms wrapped around her for warmth. "You've been out there all afternoon. Just do your business and come inside." She stomped her foot in frustration as the dog ignored her and butted the door with his head. "Bear, don't make me come get you."

He looked over his shoulder at her and woofed. Turning, he trotted across the yard to her and waited just out of reach. He barked again. When she took a step toward him, Bear whirled around and sped back to the shed, waving his tail.

Mission accomplished.

Complaining under her breath, Katie walked over. "Come on, Bear." She snagged his collar and pulled. "Enough already." Her feet skidded in the snow as she yanked harder. "Dude, it's just a tool shed." Bear twisted his neck and lunged aside, breaking free from her grasp. Standing up on his hind legs, he planted his paws on the frame and yelped again, his tail thrashing back and forth.

Katie paused. Something's in there. *A cat, maybe? I better leave the door ajar, just in case.* "Okay, Bear. You win. I'll open it, but no chasing whatever comes out. Especially if it's a skunk. Got it?" As she fumbled with the latch, the dog dropped to all fours, crowding her in his eagerness to get inside. She swung the door wide and staggered as Bear dove past her. Knocking over a rake, he nosed at a dark form pressed into the corner.

"Bear, no," whispered a hoarse voice. A hand emerged out of the gloom and pushed the dog's massive head away.

Katie gasped. Peering into the corner, she inched forward. "Griffin? Is that you?"

"Nope," he said, and coughed.

Pulling the fallen rake aside, she stepped closer and crouched down. "Oh, Griffin."

Griffin's Fire

Griffin sat huddled against the wall, shivering, his arms pulled inside his tee shirt and his bare feet tucked under a burlap bag of seeds. He glanced at her, then dropped his eyes and coughed again.

"What the heck happened? What are you doing in here?" she asked.

"Gardening."

A corner of her mouth twitched. She gazed at him for a moment, then sighed. "Are you hiding?"

He shrugged. "I didn't know where else to go." He pulled his arms free and pushed off the floor, holding onto Bear for support. "Sorry about crashing in your shed." He staggered a step, and then slumped to the ground when his knees buckled.

"Whoa there." Katie seized his arm and helped him up. "Just how long have you been out here? With no jacket?" She looked down. "And barefooted?"

"A-all afternoon," he said through chattering teeth, one hand braced on the nearby workbench. "I'll t-take off now." He started toward the door, then stopped when she tightened her grip.

"No way. You're not going anywhere except inside." Katie nodded toward the house, a line appearing between her fair brows. "We'll talk there. About everything."

His breath caught at her familiar expression. "I forgot how stubborn you are."

"I'm not stubborn, I'm freezing." Matching his unsteady steps, she led the way across the yard as Bear danced around them, panting with delight.

Once inside, Griffin groaned in relief when he collapsed on a chair. Bear pressed up against his leg. "Traitor," he murmured, tugging the dog's ear.

Wrapping his arms around his body, he squeezed his eyes tight, half listening to the sound of running water while he tried to control his shivering. He opened his eyes when Katie pressed a warm damp cloth into his hand. After wiping his grimy face and hands, he peeked up at her. "I'm surprised you're even talking to me." He handed it back to her, then bent over and coughed again, resting his head on his knees. *Oh, Fire, I feel like hammered doodoo. This is what I get for using a double shot of Elements. When will I learn?*

Katie tossed the cloth into the sink, then frowned as she studied him. "I was going to kick your butt for breaking up with me, but it looks like someone already did. Did you get in a fight with Sergei? Or someone at school?"

Griffin sat up and opened his mouth, then closed it again. *How do I tell her? That I hurt her just to save myself?* He looked away. Self-loathing flooded his mouth in a bitter wave.

Katie pulled out a chair and sat down, then took his cold hand and threaded their fingers together. "I have this friend," she began. "Who's had a bunch of horrible stuff happen to him. Even though he is this incredible guy who always tries to do the right thing. In every situation." She pulled him around to face her. "And I hope he knows that we're still friends and that he can count on me. No matter what."

"He doesn't deserve you as a friend," Griffin said roughly. "Not if he lied to you. Not if he hurt you. You shouldn't forgive him."

She smiled as tears filled her eyes. "But my friend told me once that's when you *do* forgive people. When they've hurt you the most. Because that's when it means the most."

"He sounds like a total jerk."

"No, he's not. I mean I was really upset when he did what he did. But it just wasn't him, you know? There's something going on," she said, rubbing his chilled fingers. "I think it's something bad, and he won't tell me what it is. But I know *him*. And I know that he needs one person in this world who's on his side." She sniffed and gave him a lopsided grin. "And that person is me." She let go of his hand and mopped her cheeks. "By the way, I totally practiced that speech."

Griffin stared at her for a moment, a smile spreading across his face. "I can't believe I'm sitting here with you. After everything I did." He coughed and shivered again, not just from the cold. "Well,

I'm not making that mistake again, Katie. No more lies." He slid off his chair and knelt down beside her. "I have something to tell you," he said, resting his hands on her knees. "Something wonderful." He leaned forward and whispered in her ear.

Bear leaped up and barked at Katie's cry of joy.

Chapter Thirty-Two

Katie's Journal: Friday, February 25th
If someone had told me earlier today that my boyfriend (who just happens to be an angel) would be hiding out in my bedroom in the middle of the night, I would have said: A) I don't currently have a boyfriend, B) No way would he be in my room, and C) An angel? Are you kidding me?

Shows what can happen in one day.

It's almost midnight, but I'm too wound up to sleep. I know Griffin is scared about what will happen to him, but I don't know how long I can keep him a secret from my parents.

After he told me the good news, he got ready to leave. Said he had to run away before Basil could catch him. Of course, right after that, he collapsed on the kitchen floor.

No way was I going to let him take off in the middle of a storm, angel or no angel! I remember how sick and weak he got in December using both Elements at the same time.

So between me and Bear, we managed to get him up to my room. He was asleep when he hit the mattress. I piled a spare blanket and my old sleeping bag over him, disguising him. He needed the extra warmth and it just looks like my usual messy room. It might pass if no one looks too closely. It was either that or stuff him in my closet.

Dinner took forever. I freaked each time the house creaked in the wind. Afraid it was him moving around upstairs. Luckily, Mom and Dad didn't notice anything. Except Dad wondered why Bear kept hanging out in my room. I told them I ate a roast beef sandwich in there and he must still smell it.

* * *

Katie closed her laptop and then slid it under her desk. Kicking the blanket off her legs, she rolled out of her beanbag and shuffled over to the bed on her knees. She leaned close to the lump and listened, then peeled the covers off Griffin's face, his features barely discernible in the dark.

"Hey," she whispered. "You awake?" She smiled at the faint grunt. "Do you want some more water?"

Griffin licked his dry lips and nodded. Uncurling, he rolled over onto his back and sat up. He propped himself against the headboard as Katie stuffed the pillow behind him. "Thanks," he said, his hand trembling as he took the proffered bottle. He struggled to unscrew the lid.

"Here. Let me get that." Katie eased down next to him and removed the top, then helped him take a few sips. "How are you feeling now?"

"Not as wiped out. Still tired, though, from using both my Elements at same time." He knuckled his eyes and yawned, his jaw popping, then looked around. "Have you been awake all night?"

"I'm too excited to sleep," she said, picking at a hole in the knee of her worn sweatpants. "Anyway, someone's hogging the bed." She grinned and reached out to smooth his rumpled hair off his forehead. "Not that I mind." Her smile faded when she glanced over at the closed door. "But if my parents were to walk in here right now..." She stopped and drew her finger across her throat, then took his hand and squeezed it. "Are you *sure* you don't want to tell Basil?"

"No, Katie, I'm not sure. I'm not sure about anything." He pulled her over and tucked her under his arm. As she snuggled next to him, he rubbed his chin against her silky hair. "I don't know what to do." He snorted. "Here I am—a guardian angel. On the run from *other* guardian angels because I want to *stay* a guardian angel. And I'm hiding out in my human girlfriend's bedroom. In the middle of the night. While her parents are across the hall asleep." He shook his head. "Talk about one screwed up life. Plus." Griffin pulled the neck of his tee shirt up to his nose. "I smell really bad." He grinned and held out his free hand, flexing it while he examined his bruised knuckles. "But it sure felt good to pound Sergei. Of course he got in a few hits, too." He winced as he rubbed his jaw.

A thrill shot through him when Katie traced the muscles in his arm. "I always knew you could take him." She stilled her hand and cleared her throat. "Did you know about him? Coming over and talking with me? Trying to get me interested in him?"

"I'm aware," he said, shifting uncomfortably.

"You planned all that?"

"Sergei was the mastermind, but, yeah, I had to go along with it." He looked at her. "I'm sorry, Katie. I'm so sorry. I just freaked out when he said he was going to tell Basil."

She laid a finger on his lips. "Ssssh. Not so loud," she whispered. "Look, you explained everything and..." She stopped when Griffin tensed and held up a hand, his head cocked to one side. Listening. They froze at the creak outside the door, their eyes mirroring each other's alarm. After a long minute of silence, they relaxed and sighed in relief.

"Old house," Griffin said with a shrug. "Now, where were we?"

"You were groveling for forgiveness, I believe." They laughed, trying to stifle the sound.

Still chuckling, Katie reached around and grabbed the water off the nightstand. "Here—finish this. Do you want anything to eat?"

He chugged the rest and wiped his mouth. "That'd be great. It'll help me get my energy back." He handed the empty bottle to her. "And some more water, please?"

"You got it." She started to clamber over him, then squeaked when he snagged her around the waist and pulled her back into his lap.

"Before you go," he said, drawing his blanket-covered knees up and cradling her in his arms. "I need to say something." He tucked her hair behind one ear and stroked her cheek with his thumb as he gazed down into her face. "Thank you."

"For what?"

"What do you think?" He smiled. "For being Katie." He tightened his arms as he started to kiss her.

At that moment, the door swung open.

Chapter Thirty-Three

"Where on earth can he be?" Basil muttered, appearing in a whirlwind of snow in his backyard. Striding across the yard toward the house, his face hardened at the sight of Sergei working by the light from the kitchen as he re-attached the door. Tools lay scattered around the patio. "Aren't you finished yet?"

"No, sir." Sergei bent over and tightened the next screw on the bottom hinge, his eyes fixed on his task.

"When you are, the kitchen needs to be cleaned."

"Yes, sir."

"No sign of him yet?"

"No, sir."

Basil stood watching. "I'm still trying to decide which one of you I'm more infuriated with—Griffin for not telling me or you for blackmailing him." He hid a smile when Sergei fidgeted under his scrutiny. "And just how long were you two going to continue this deception, eh?" Before Sergei could answer, a low chime sounded from Basil's pocket. He dug his cell phone out. "This conversation is far from over, Tiro." Stepping around Sergei, he headed inside. "Hello?"

"Basil?" Helen' voice held more than a trace of amusement. "Are you, by any chance, missing anything? Or anyone?"

While she described the scene, Basil closed his eyes as he listened. "Right, Helen, and thank you. I'll be over directly."

Tucking his phone away, he hurried through the house toward the front door and flung it open. He stared at the Heflin's home. Lights blazed from every window.

Basil walked down the steps and across the empty street, the storm clouds lifting overhead. He shook his head. *Thank Heaven, the lad's safe*, he thought as he reached the far sidewalk. *I wonder what Lewis' reaction was when he discovered Fin in Katie's—*

As that moment, the Heflin's front door flew opened. Griffin barreled out and stumbled down the steps. Backpedaling across the yard on bare feet, he tried to calm a furious Lewis storming after him.

"Mr. Heflin, it wasn't like that—I swear! I was just..."

"And then I walk into my daughter's bedroom and what do I find? YOU! In her bed! In the middle of the night! Doing who knows what," Lewis raged, refusing to listen. His robe flapped over his pajamas as he shook off Helen's restraining hand on his arm. Katie yelled at her father to stop.

Griffin backed up a few more steps to the middle of the yard, unsure what to do next. He frowned in confusion when he noticed Katie mouthing something. She gestured frantically over his shoulder. He whirled around.

And bumped into Basil.

With a gasp, he looked up into his Mentor's face. For a moment, they stared at each other.

"Oh, Fire." Griffin dodged to one side as Basil suddenly lunged for him. Skidding in the snow, he stumbled once, then turned and raced back toward the Heflin's house.

"Griffin! Wait, lad. I must tell you..." Basil cursed under his breath and bolted after him. As they neared the house, both angels vanished in a spray of snow, powdering the Heflins as they watched from the porch.

"Where did they go?" Lewis asked.

Darby Karchut

Biting her lip, Katie studied the double set of footprints ending at the bottom of the steps. She looked up. "They're headed for the back yard."

Katie dashed inside, her parents on her heels. Racing down the hall, they tore through the kitchen. Bear raged inside his kennel, biting at the metal gate. Helen stopped to unlatch the gate. She stepped aside as he shot out the back door after Katie.

Helen joined them on the patio, pulling her robe tight around her neck as she wrapped an arm around her shivering daughter. Lewis grabbed the dog's collar and held the wolfhound close while they all looked up at the sky. A star peeped through a band of clouds streaming eastward. A silence, like a breath held in wonder, filled the air.

With a shout of triumph, Basil appeared, holding a struggling Griffin around the chest. "Steady on, Fin." He winced as Griffin's elbow jabbed him in the ribs. "You're not going anywhere until we have a chance to talk."

"Let me go." Griffin thrashed from side to side as he fought Basil's iron clutch. "I won't go mortal again. I won't. I'll die first." With a desperate effort, he braced his feet and twisted free. Spinning around, he flung out both arms in a wild gesture. With a roar, a wall of Fire exploded between them.

"Oh, come now. That's scarcely an adequate defensive," Basil said, his face half hidden by the flames. "Considering I'm the one who taught you that particular maneuver." He lifted his hands. Water jetted from his fingertips as he doused the blaze; the melting snow pooled underfoot. "I quite understand you're upset, but there is no need for this..." He paused when Griffin stamped the ground in front of him, slush and mud spraying out from under his foot. A deep crevasse ripped the ground open with a groan, as if it objected to be awakened in the dead of winter. Basil raised an eyebrow as it raced toward him. "...for this belligerence."

"I'm warning you, Basil. I *will* fight you." Chest heaving, Griffin shifted his body into battle stance, certain he would lose. He blinked in confusion when the Mentor stopped and looked down, stroking his chin.

"Is this a new skill?" Basil stepped over the ditch with his long stride and walked around, examining the ground. "So, tell me—must you be barefooted to do this? Or have you tried it with shoes on?"

Griffin narrowed his eyes in suspicion as he edged away. "W-what are you talking about?"

"I'm talking about your newest technique, you thick-headed Tiro. And I must say I'm delighted you've kept up with your training." He looked up with a growing smile. "Even so, I imagine we've some remediation to do, eh? After all, I can't have my apprentice lagging behind the other Senior Tiros, now can I?"

"Your T-Ti..."

Basil nodded. "Yes, *Tiro*, you dolt. That's what I've been attempting to tell you." Stepping closer, he bent his head and murmured softly for a few minutes.

Griffin turned away, one hand covering his face. Basil wrapped an arm around his apprentice's shoulders. Glancing over at Helen, they exchanged looks, then she nodded and shooed her family inside, Katie sobbing with joy. Basil smiled his thanks and gazed up the stars. After a while, a muffled voice spoke from somewhere around his elbow.

"Basil?"

"Fin."

Griffin raised his head. He sniffed as he dragged his arm across his nose. "You know what this means?"

"Tell me, lad."

Lifting his face, Griffin watched as the last of the clouds shredded away, revealing a diamond-dusted sky. He closed his eyes and shouted in exultation. "No more algebra!"

Darby Karchut

Chapter Thirty-Four

Griffin's Journal: Saturday, February 26th
I wish I had told Katie the truth earlier. It would have saved her and me a butt-load of grief. But she seemed okay with why I kept it a secret.

And Basil. I don't understand why he doesn't just give up on me? Especially since I screwed up everything so bad.

So badly.

When I asked him that very question, he just smiled and said giving up was not in his nature.

True that.

Basil's Journal: Tuesday, March 1st
Griffin and I both learned an invaluable lesson: secrets can hurt those whom you love, even when kept for the finest of reasons.

Fin's reversal (for lack of a better phrase—I refuse to use the term 'born again') has the other Terrae Angeli, especially Flight Command, in an uproar as to the how and the why. (Although Sukalli is secretly pleased. He still feels guilty for his role in all this even though he has proven himself a staunch friend.)

Of course, Fin and I have our own humble theory of how and why he is a Terrae Angelus again. An assumption that seems to be quite out of favor in this day and age:

That it was by grace.

And grace alone.

Katie's Journal: Friday, March 4th

Griffin's prayers came true.

He'll be a Terrae Angelus. Maybe for thousands of years. Maybe forever.

But I will grow up. Go to college. Get married. Have children. Have a career. Then I will age. Grow old. Grow older. And then I'll die.

And Griffin will stay Griffin.

So that's good.

So why do I feel so sad?

Chapter Thirty-Five

Griffin stepped in front of Mrs. Heflin's Volkswagen. Laying his hands on its hood, he bowed his head; his lips moved in silent prayer. He flinched and looked up when the horn squawked.

Katie stuck her head out the driver's side window and glared at him. "You are *so* not funny," she said, turning on the ignition. "Now get in."

"Do I have to?" Griffin walked around to the passenger's side of the tiny car and peered in the open window, stalling for time. "Can't I just meet you there? I mean, you've only had your license a few days."

"Chicken."

"You got that right. I'm not immortal, you know. I *can* be killed."

"*I'm* going to kill you if you don't get in this car." Katie shifted the transmission into drive. "So move your butt, angel boy."

"I love it when you talk like that." With a grin, Griffin slid into his seat. He clutched the armrest as they lurched away from the curb and headed out of their neighborhood; he hurriedly put on his seat belt. "Thanks again for swinging by Cas' before we head over to Miss Lena's."

"No problem. Now don't talk to me. I need to concentrate." She clutched the wheel with both hands as they entered High Springs' downtown, its streets frantic with morning traffic. She gasped when the truck ahead of her veered into her lane, almost clipping the car's front fender. It roared away in a cloud of blue smoke.

"*Libera nos a malo*," Griffin muttered under his breath.

"What's that mean?"

"It's Latin for 'deliver us from evil.'"

"Of course it is." Shifting in her seat, she frowned as she noticed him scanning the street on either side. "What are you doing?"

"Oh, just keeping an eye on things."

"Aren't you off duty right now?"

"Well, yeah. But that doesn't mean anything." He craned his neck as they passed a schoolyard, checking out a basketball game in progress. "I'm always on call. In a way."

A creeping realization nudged at Katie. She pushed it away. Fixing a smile on her face, she pulled up to the curb in front of Cas' house. Jumping out before Griffin could help her, she waited while he retrieved the book from under his seat.

As they made their way up the walkway, the front door swung open. A small figure in pink overalls raced out.

"Gwiffin!" Tessie shouted, running as fast as her tiny legs could move.

"Here—hold this for me." Griffin handed the book to Katie. He braced himself as the little girl plowed into him and flung her arms around one of his legs. "Help," he cried, flailing his arms in mock terror. "There's a monster attacking me. The Tessie monster. Oh, no." As she shrieked with laughter, he peeled her away and took her hand.

At that moment, Cas appeared in the doorway. "Hey, guys," he said as he walked toward them. He swatted at Griffin's stomach with the back of his hand. "Missed you in history. How do you like being a free man?"

Griffin blocked his friend's blow. "How do you think?" He took the book from Katie and handed it to Cas. "Hey, can you drop this off at the school library for me? I forgot to bring it back when I withdrew. Tell Mrs. Guthrie thanks for me."

"I'll take care of it on Monday. You want to come in?"

"Nah, but thanks. We're going to help a friend move today." He handed Tessie off.

Cas nodded as he took his sister's arm. "By the way, did you hear about Milton?"

"What—he bullied the wrong student and got fired?"

"How did you know?" At their stunned expressions, Cas continued. "I overheard my dad talking to my mom. From what I understand, Milton had been picking on some freshman all year. You know, making fun of him in front of the class, pushing him around, stuff like that. I guess Milton finally lost it and hit the guy. So the guy complained to the principal. Then his parents got involved. So now Milton is suspended. And yeah, he might even get fired."

"Good," Katie said with a curl of her lip. "I hope he ends up washing cars the rest of his life."

"What about the guy?" Griffin asked.

Cas frowned. "What do you mean?"

"I mean, is anyone going to help *him*?"

"Why would he need any help? I mean, he had a rough year, but Milton's gone now. It's all over."

No, Griffin thought. *No, it's not over.* "Say, Cas? Could you get me the name of that freshman?"

"Sure, but why?"

"Oh, I just want to talk with him."

* * *

"And that next box goes in here, Katie," Lena said from her position in the middle of the living room. She crossed off the item on her clipboard and stored the pencil behind her ear. "Put it down by the sofa. I'll unpack it later."

"What's in it?" Katie set the box down on the floor and slid it into the corner with her foot. "Sound like dishes or something."

"Why, it's my angel figurines."

Griffin's Fire

"Oh, do you collect them?"

Lena glanced around, then leaned closer. "Personally, I find them a bit absurd. But certain Terrae Angeli insist on gifting them to me." She looked at the box wistfully. "I was hoping you might drop it by accident."

They stepped aside as Griffin edged into the living room backwards, juggling his half of a tall cabinet. "That goes in the corner by the fireplace, *liebling*."

He grunted, angling it around the corner. The muscles on his forearms strained as he gripped the massive shelving. "Maybe we should have come in through the patio." He hissed when he skinned his knuckles on the doorframe.

"Maybe you should stop talking and pay attention to what you're about," Basil said, appearing on the tail end. He lifted his side of the cabinet over a stray box, then hauled it over to the corner. "Right. Lower yours down, Fin. Careful, now."

They eased the shelf upright, pushed it in place, and then sighed in unison. Griffin sucked on his bleeding knuckle while Basil dusted his hands on his worn sweatshirt.

"Good. Now I can park in my new garage." Lena tucked the clipboard under her arm. "Next on the agenda is lunch. Katie, you'll help, yes?" She wrapped an arm around the girl's waist and escorted her to the kitchen.

Griffin pushed his damp hair off his forehead. "Finally—I'm starving." He started to follow them when Basil snagged his arm.

"In a minute. Let's talk about tonight."

"Why? Is there a problem?" At Basil's gesture, he took a seat on a box of books. "I mean, Command cleared me for missions, didn't they?"

Basil leaned an elbow on the fireplace mantel. "They did. I simply wanted to make sure you feel ready." He raised an eyebrow in question. "After all, you've been through quite a trial by fire. No pun intended."

Griffin grinned. "Ready and able," he said. "You know, this'll be my first mission as a Senior Tiro."

"And Sergei?"

"What about him?" His smile faded as he looked down and picked at the tape on the lid. "He's not coming along, is he?"

"Not this time, no." Basil walked over and took a seat on a nearby chair. "But despite everything, I am his Mentor, too. And I have a responsibility to him as well as you."

"He's an ass."

"Enough of that, lad," Basil admonished. "Sergei may not have the most stellar personality, but he's a remarkably gifted Terrae Angelus. And we need him. And you. Trained and promoted as soon as possible. You know this."

"Yeah."

"So, until he's gone, I require a truce between you two. And I want it to begin with you."

Griffin made a face. "Why me?"

Basil reached over and patted his Tiro's knee. "Because I've always been able to count on you to do the right thing." Standing up, he cuffed Griffin lightly on the head before hauling him upright and pushing him toward the kitchen. "Sans the episode in Katie's bedroom. Just what in Heaven's name were you thinking? You very nearly gave Lewis a stroke."

"For the hundredth time—we weren't doing *anything*," protested Griffin. "I was asleep in her bed practically the whole night." He glared over his shoulder at his Mentor.

Basil winced. "It sounds worse every time you say it."

* * *

"Thanks for helping us move Miss Lena. Sorry you had to give up your Saturday," Griffin said, holding Katie's hands while they lingered on her porch.

"At least we got to be together some more. I miss seeing you at school."

"I know. That's the only bad part of all this." He glanced across the street at a familiar whistle; he nodded when he saw Basil point upward with a meaningful look before disappearing inside.

"Are you on call now?" Katie asked, a faint line appearing between her brows.

"Yup." He reached over, smoothing the frown away with his thumb. "And stop worrying."

She wrapped her arms around his waist as she gazed up into his eyes. "Promise me you won't get hurt."

"I can't. All I can promise you is that I'll do what is needed." He shook his head when she started to argue. "It's who I am, Katie. It's why I was created. To sacrifice *everything* for you mortals if necessary."

"I know," she said with a sigh. "And I love that about you." *And I hate that about you.*

"See you tomorrow." He kissed her goodbye and then hurried across the street. Taking the porch steps two at a time, he slipped inside.

Opening his mouth to holler his arrival, he clapped his jaw shut at the sound of a strange voice coming from the living room. He eased the door closed, then crept across the hall and peeked around the corner.

A dark-haired figure, a week's worth of stubble on his lean jaw and his khaki clothing rumpled and sand-stained, stood in the middle of the room with Sergei hovering by his side. He finished shaking Basil's hand.

"I would have contacted you to explain the situation," said the stranger, "but it seemed simpler to just come and tell you directly. Plus I wanted to surprise Sergei. I hope you don't mind."

"Of course not," Basil said. "Will you be taking your Tiro back with you to the Middle East?"

"No, thank Heaven—we're returning home to Denver. And now that the situation in that region is somewhat stabilized, Command has found someone to replace me. I believe you know him—Nicopolis?"

Darby Karchut

Basil's eyebrows shot up. "I do."

"Well, he seemed less than enthusiastic about the mission." The stranger tilted his head. "A friend of yours?"

"No, not really."

The stranger started to say something, then changed the subject. "Anyway, as soon as I got the all clear, I took off." He clapped a hand on Sergei's shoulder. "I swear he's grown another inch." His eyes widened as he looked past Sergei and spied Griffin in the archway. "And you must be..."

"Yes, sir." Griffin eased into the room. "I'm Griffin." He almost added *Raine*, but stopped himself in time.

"Mentor Dimitri," the stranger replied, looking Griffin up and down. "I was interested in meeting you."

"Sir?"

"News travels fast. You're quite the curiosity now. Angel to mortal to angel again." He looked over at Basil. "And I assume everything went smoothly with my Tiro."

Basil hesitated for a moment, and then gestured with his head toward the hall. "Griffin, go upstairs and help Sergei pack, eh?"

Meaning he wants to talk to Mentor Dimitri privately. "Yes, sir." Griffin headed upstairs with the other Tiro on his heels.

Sergei crowded past and hurried into his room. While Griffin watched from the doorway, he pulled his duffle bag out from under the bed and dumped it on top. Yanking open drawers, he grabbed shirts and jeans, wadding them up and stuffing them in the bag. He checked the closet, grabbed his other pair of shoes, and threw them in as well.

Oh, come on. You can pack faster than that. "Don't forget your junk in the bathroom," Griffin said aloud, and then crept across the corridor to the railing, trying to listen. *I hope he tells Mentor Dimitri everything*, he thought, leaning over to hear better.

He jumped when a laden duffle thudded to the floor behind him. Whirling around, he tensed as Sergei stepped closer.

The other Tiro stared at him, a strange expression on his face. "Look," he said after a moment. "Basil's been fair with me—so I owe him. And I think he'd want me to say this to you."

"What are you talking—"

"You put up a good fight. I couldn't get past those fireballs of yours. Maybe I was wrong about you." Sergei shrugged. "But maybe not. Because I still think you're a worthless excuse of a Tiro with some serious self-esteem issues."

"And you're still an arrogant know-it-all with delusions of godhood."

Sergei thought for a moment, then a corner of his mouth curled up. "True that." Without another word, he grabbed his gear and walked away.

Stunned by the other Tiro's words, Griffin lingered in the corridor as he listened to their goodbyes to Basil, the door closing shortly afterwards. Then he headed down.

"Okay, that was beyond weird," he said, meeting his Mentor at the foot of the stairs. "Even for us. Mentor Dimitri showing up like that out of the blue."

"'Deus ex machina,' eh?"

"What's that...no, wait." Griffin raised his hand in protest when his Mentor opened his mouth to explain. "On second thought, I'll just look it up."

"Good choice." Basil gestured toward the back of the house. "We best eat while we can. How about leftover tuna casserole for our resident Earth and Fire?"

Griffin made a gagging noise as he followed Basil down the hall and into the kitchen. "What are *you* having?"

"Well..." Basil opened the refrigerator and scratched his head. He stood there a few moments, and then shut the door and walked over to the phone. "What the speed dial number for Giuseppe's Pizza?"

Darby Karchut

"Six. And I want the veggie with pineapples. No onions," Griffin said, piling books to one side of the table. He plopped a roll of paper towels in the middle of it. "There. All set."

Basil chuckled while he waited on hold and motioned Griffin over. He held the phone up to his ear. "They're playing your theme song."

Griffin listened for a moment. "Oh, just great. Now I'm going to have that tune stuck in my head all night."

"I thought you enjoyed Johnny Cash?"

"I do, but after a bazillion times of Ring of Fire, even *I'm* getting..." He stopped when the Light pierced the kitchen. His pulse began to race as the urgent voice spoke.

When the beam faded away, they turned in unison and sprinted through the house to the entryway. Basil snagged both jackets from the hooks. Tossing one to Griffin, he flung the door open. They stepped outside.

"Remember, Tiro..."

"I know, I know. Check both ways before take off."

Basil laughed. "Cheeky." With a nod, he sprinted across the porch and leaped off the top step. Griffin vaulted one-handed over the railing a second behind him.

Together, they vanished into the evening sky.

Griffin's Fire

Chapter Thirty-Six

The girl leaned back against the car's windshield as she sat on the hood, her legs stretched out before her. She held up the pill container and gave it a shake. It rattled, more than half full.

The leftover heat from the engine warmed her against the chill of the spring evening. Glancing around the deserted parking lot, she drained the beer can clutched in her other hand and tossed it away.

"God, I hope I don't screw *this* up like everything else in my life," she murmured, twisting the lid off the container. Tiny white pills, like baby teeth, spilled out into her hand. She placed one tablet after another along a jean-clad leg. While she stared at the first sleeping pill, trying to work up her nerve, a gust blew her hair across her face. She jumped at the sound of someone clearing their throat.

"Um, hi there," said a voice.

She gasped and whipped her head around, the pills sliding off her leg. A teen boy stood a few yards away.

"Sorry I scared you. I guess I came in a little too fast. I'm out of practice." He shook his dark hair out of his eyes and strolled nearer.

"What the hell do *you* want?" she asked, her fingers scrambling beside her knee for the pills.

"To help you."

Darby Karchut

"I don't need any help so get lost." She looked down, searching frantically before her courage slipped away. When she looked up, he was still there, an odd expression on his face. "What?" she asked in exasperation.

"I'm not leaving. Not until I've saved you. It's why I was assigned here." He waved his hand around. For a moment, the girl thought she saw tiny flames shoot out of the tips of his fingers. "Oops!" He made a fist and dropped his arm. "As I was saying, it's sort of my job."

"Your job."

"That's right."

"To save me."

"Yup."

"What are you, one of those church guys?"

"No. Actually, I am a junior member of the ancient order of the Terrae Angeli—supernatural first responders for mortals in danger." He rattled it off as if he had said it dozens of times.

"Wait. What?" She shook her head, as if clearing her ears. "Are you some kind of nut case?"

"Nope, I'm a kind of angel." He grinned. "Cool, huh?"

"Riiight."

"No, really."

"So if angels really exist, how come I've never seen one?" Before he could speak, she held up a hand. "Let me guess. 'Only dogs...'"

"'...and small children,'" he finished. "You've heard the old wives' tale, too."

The girl blinked. For a blinding second, a forgotten memory from her childhood exploded in her mind. A memory of a pair of hands catching her when she tumbled off the highest rung of the monkey bars. Of looking up into eyes as blue as the sky. Then finding herself safely on her feet, seeing only an empty playground and hearing the whisper of an amused voice tickling her ear. *Dogs and small children, eh, lass?*

Griffin's Fire

Something shifted inside of her. A tiny crack opened.

She fought back against the hope peeking in. "You're crazy, dude. Angels aren't real."

To her surprise, he shrugged. "Well, maybe they aren't. I mean, that would be insanely weird." He stepped closer and lowered his voice, as if sharing a secret. "But wouldn't it be worth sticking around *this* life a little longer?"

"Why?" she whispered, the crack inside of her widening.

He smiled, his brown eyes crinkling at the corners, and held out his hand to help her down. "Why, just to find out."

Author's Notes

As I mentioned previously in the first book in the series, *Griffin Rising*, it was in the summer of 2009 that I came across an obscure and rather brief description from the Middle Ages about a lower caste of angels. According to tradition, these angels, besides acting as guardians, were also said to control the four elements of earth, fire, wind, and water. And thus, Griffin, Basil, and the other Terrae Angeli were born.

However, the belief in supernatural or angelic beings can be found in many of the world's religions and is not limited to Christianity. I borrowed from Judaism as well as Islam, Hinduism, and even ancient Babylon

In addition to religious influences, I've also added bits and pieces from other cultures and historical events. Touches of classical Sparta, the Irish myths of Cuchulainn, Finn and the Red Branch, the European feudal system, the Plains Indians of North America, and Great Britain's Royal Air Force during World War Two all found their way into Griffin's tale.

And with the introduction of Sergei, I gave a nod to the Cold War of the twentieth century between the Soviet Union (now known as Russia) and the United States. The parallel between that Cold War and Griffin and Sergei's conflict was completely and utterly intentional.

You think I just make this stuff up?

Acknowledgments

Griffin has introduced me to so many incredible people: Brooke Johnson, whose friendship and critiquing skills have been a true-blue blessing; Beverly Stowe McClure, Susan Goldsmith, Jennifer Murgia, and C. Lee McKenzie, fellow authors and as classy as they come.

Once again, I wish to thank my family (Wes, Mom, Kelly, Derek, Lee, Robin, Roshelle, Dad, and Harlene), and friends (Debbi, Kaci, Molly, Stephanie, Greg, Lori, Tiffany, Ashley, Todd, Amy, Lynn, Gwen, Beth, Jeff, and the other faculty members and students at Cheyenne Mountain Junior High), who politely refrained from sticking their fingers in their ears and humming loudly when they saw me coming.

I bow before the awesomeness known as books bloggers: Tracy, Kelly, Katie, Carmel, Melissa, Jamie, Naj, Jenny, AimeeKay, Kathy, Amelia, and all the others who helped spread the word. And most importantly, thank you to the many readers who have befriended Griffin and Basil.

Angels all.

Darby Karchut

About the Author

Darby Karchut is a best selling and award-winning author, dreamer, and compulsive dawn greeter. She's been known to run in blizzards and bike in lightning storms. When not dodging death by Colorado, Darby writes urban fantasy for tweens, teens, and adults. Visit her at www.darbykarchut.com

Othe Books by Darby Karchut

Young Adult
Griffin Rising - Book One
Griffin's Fire - Book Two
Griffin's Storm - Book Three

The Adventures of Finn MacCullen
(Spencer Hill Middle Grade)
Finn Finnegan - Book One
(2014 IPPY Silver Medal)
Gideon's Spear - Book Two
The Hound at the Gate - Book Three

Non-Fiction
Money and Teens: Savvy Money Skills
(with Wes Karchut)

Writing as Darby Kaye
The Stag Lord - 2014 from Spence City
Unholy Blue - 2015 from Spence City

Darby Karchut

www.ingramcontent.com/pod-product-compliance
Lightning Source LLC
Chambersburg PA
CBHW061640040426
42446CB00010B/1511